Better Days

by Richard Dresser

SAMUEL FRENCH, INC.
45 WEST 25TH STREET   NEW YORK 10010
7623 SUNSET BOULEVARD   HOLLYWOOD 90046
LONDON   *TORONTO*

Copyright © 1988, 1991 by Richard Dresser

ALL RIGHTS RESERVED

CAUTION: Professionals and amateurs are hereby warned that BETTER DAYS is subject to a royalty. It is fully protected under the copyright laws of the United States of America, the British Commonwealth, including Canada, and all other countries of the Copyright Union. All rights, including professional, amateur, motion pictures, recitation, lecturing, public reading, radio broadcasting, television, and the rights of translation into foreign languages are strictly reserved. In its present form the play is dedicated to the reading public only.

The amateur live stage performance rights to BETTER DAYS are controlled exclusively by Samuel French, Inc., and royalty arrangements and licenses must be secured well in advance of presentation. PLEASE NOTE that amateur royalty fees are set upon application in accordance with your producing circumstances. When applying for a royalty quotation and license please give us the number of performances intended, dates of production, your seating capacity and admission fee. Royalties are payable one week before the opening performance of the play to Samuel French, Inc., at 45 W. 25th Street, New York, NY 10010; or at 7623 Sunset Blvd., Hollywood, CA 90046, or to Samuel French (Canada), Ltd., 80 Richmond Street East, Toronto, Ontario, Canada M5C 1P1.

Royalty of the required amount must be paid whether the play is presented for charity or gain and whether or not admission is charged.

Stock royalty quoted on application to Samuel French, Inc.

For all other rights than those stipulated above, apply to George P. Lane, c/o William Morris Agency, Inc., 1350 Avenue of the Americas, New York, NY 10019.

Particular emphasis is laid on the question of amateur or professional readings, permission and terms for which must be secured in writing from Samuel French, Inc.

Copying from this book in whole or in part is strictly forbidden by law, and the right of performance is not transferable.

Whenever the play is produced the following notice must appear on all programs, printing and advertising for the play: "Produced by special arrangement with Samuel French, Inc."

Due authorship credit must be given on all programs, printing and advertising for the play.

ISBN 0 573 69261 0   Printed in U.S.A.

No one shall commit or authorize any act or omission by which the copyright of, or the right to copyright, this play may be impaired.

No one shall make any changes in this play for the purpose of production.

Publication of this play does not imply availability for performance. Both amateurs and professionals considering a production are *strongly* advised in their own interests to apply to Samuel French, Inc., for written permission before starting rehearsals, advertising, or booking a theatre.

No part of this book may be reproduced, stored in a retrieval system, or transmitted in any form, by any means, now known or yet to be invented, including mechanical, electronic, photocopying, recording, videotaping, or otherwise, without the prior written permission of the publisher.

IMPORTANT BILLING AND CREDIT REQUIREMENTS

All producers of BETTER DAYS *must* give credit to the Author of the Play in all programs distributed in connection with performances of the Play and in all instances in which the title of the Play appears for purposes of advertising, publicizing or otherwise exploiting the Play and/or a production. The name of the Author *must* also appear on a separate line, on which no other name appears, immediately following the title, and *must* appear in size of type not less than fifty percent the size of the title type.

Better Days premiered April 7, 1987 at the Philadelphia Festival Theatre for New Plays with the following cast (in order of appearance):

RAY..Frank Girardeau
ARNIE...Stephen Bradbury
FAYE..Jayne Haynes
PHIL..James Gleason
CRYSTAL ....Jennifer Houlton
BILL...Jude Ciccolella

Directed by: Gloria Muzio
Settings by: Eric Schaeffer
Lighting by: Curt Senie
Costumes by: Vickie Esposito McLaughlin
Sound by: Jeff Chestek
Production Stage Manager: Adrienne Neye

Better Days was subsequently produced by Primary Stages, Inc. in New York City with the following cast (in order of appearance):

RAY..Daniel Ahearn
ARNIE...Kevin McClarnon
FAYE...Susan Greenhill
PHIL..James Gleason
CRYSTAL .... Ann Talman
BILL...Larry Pine

Directed by: John Pynchon Holms
Scenery by: Ray Recht
Lighting by: Steve Shelley
Costumes by: Amanda J. Klein
Sound by: Tom Gould
Production Stage Manager: Randy Lawson

CHARACTERS

RAY, mid-thirties

ARNIE, mid-thirties

FAYE, Ray's wife, mid-thirties

PHIL, mid-thirties

CRYSTAL, about twenty

BILL, forties

SETTING

The action takes place in Ray's home in a dying mill-town in New England. The playing area is the living room and the kitchen. We see the roof of the building, and through a window is the town beyond. The house seems patched together with linoleum and plywood in a hurried effort to stave off decay. Plastic coverings take the place of storm windows. A door leads outside and another door leads to the other rooms in the house. The ramshackle furniture includes a sofa and some chairs huddled around a grate where heat comes up from the furnace in the basement. It's the dead of winter.

ACT I

Scene 1

(Dusk. The living room is in half-light. RAY and ARNIE are slumped on the sofa, beer in hand, surrounded by empty beer cans. They are staring vacantly ahead, the picture of boredom. ARNIE tips his beer can all the way up to drink and taps on the bottom of the can to get every drop. Long pause.)

RAY. You want another beer, Arnie?

ARNIE. I don't know. *(Pause.)* What about you? You want another beer?

RAY. Yeah, I guess.

ARNIE. Ray? I been thinking.

RAY. Yeah?

ARNIE. Well ... aw ... skip it.

RAY. Okay.

ARNIE. *(Pause.)* What time you got?

RAY. *(Looks at his watch, shakes it, shrugs.)* I don't know.

ARNIE. Okay, maybe one more. What the hell.

RAY. *(Crushing his beer can and tossing it aside.)* I'll get 'em. *(RAY makes no move to get up.)*

ARNIE. You gettin' the beer, Ray?

RAY. Sure. I'll get 'em. *(Pause. RAY slowly goes to the kitchen.)*

ARNIE. Ray? I been thinking.

(RAY opens the refrigerator door and we see him in the ghostly light from inside the refrigerator. HE gets the beer, closes the refrigerator, glances out the window, and suddenly comes to life.)

RAY. Shit! She's comin'!

ARNIE. You said she was out tonight.

RAY. She was but she ain't now. *(RAY comes out to the living room. RAY and ARNIE hurriedly try to gather up the beer cans to make the place presentable. It's hopeless.)* Cover for me, Arnie, there's stuff I was s'posed to do.

(RAY exits to the bedroom. ARNIE is alone in the living room. The door opens and FAYE enters, carrying a bag of take-out food. SHE turns on the light, revealing the full extent of the squalor.)

FAYE. Hi, Arnie.

ARNIE. Oh, hi. It's you.

FAYE. You don't mind me barging into my own house, do you?

ARNIE. No, that's fine. You're always welcome here.

FAYE. Thanks. *(FAYE takes off her coat. She's dressed as a Pilgrim.)*

ARNIE. Ray said you were going to your sister's.

FAYE. She's sick.

ARNIE. Nothing serious, I hope.

FAYE. No, just sick, like everybody gets.

ARNIE. Tough day?

FAYE. They all are. Ten lousy bucks in tips and I busted my ass for 'em. You know how long we've been eating this slop from the Hungry Pilgrim? Three weeks, Arnie.

ARNIE. Least you're working.

FAYE. They cut back on staff so we don't even clean up anymore. The owner's living in the kitchen. There's dirty clothes next to the grill, he entertains women on the cutting board, and now the refrigerator's broke so the food's going bad. (*Beat.*) Hey, you want some fried clams?

(*SHE hands him the bag of food. HE smells it and hands it back.*)

ARNIE. No thanks. I'm probably gonna eat later.

FAYE. I know, the food isn't even worth stealing anymore. I hate that place. You guys lose again?

ARNIE. Worse than ever. They killed us.

FAYE. Who was it this time?

ARNIE. There's only two teams left in the league. Us and them.

FAYE. Al's Donuts?

ARNIE. Me and Ray were the only ones on our team that showed. Least it's cheaper bowling during the day.

FAYE. Almost makes the lay-offs worthwhile.

ARNIE. It's not so bad. They gotta open up the plant again.

FAYE. You really think so?

ARNIE. Spring at the latest. That's what Ray says.

FAYE. I hope to God I can hold on that long. Every day I want less and less and every day it gets farther away.

What are we gonna do, Arnie? We can't go on like this much longer. (*Suddenly.*) Where is he?

ARNIE. Who?

FAYE. Ray. My husband.

ARNIE. Oh, him. Ray. Well, he had to go out for a while. Check on some things.

FAYE. Maybe you can help me out.

ARNIE. Anything you want, Faye.

FAYE. Bring the TV over by the door.

ARNIE. The TV? You taking it someplace?

FAYE. That's right. I'm taking it someplace.

(RAY enters.)

FAYE. I thought you were out.

RAY. You know better than that.

FAYE. Some day you guys must have had.

RAY. They're all the same now. You make a lot of money today?

FAYE. I haven't seen such cheap-skates since you used to take me out.

RAY. That's going back a ways.

FAYE. Things are gonna change around here. Starting now.

RAY. Some drinking happened. I won't deny it. I thought you were at your sister's and I had time to clean up the place.

FAYE. I guess there just aren't enough hours in the day. You do the laundry like I asked?

RAY. It's in the bedroom.

(FAYE exits to the bedroom. RAY opens the bag of take-out food and starts to eat. HE unfolds the newspaper that the food was wrapped in and tries to read it.)

ARNIE. So maybe we better call it off for tonight.

RAY. What are you talking about?

ARNIE. We can't do anything with her around.

RAY. I'll take care of it.

ARNIE. The actual thing is, I'm not exactly sure I can make it tonight.

RAY Arnie, don't talk like this. We got the full moon.

ARNIE. Betty, you know, she stays in a lot—

RAY. You're telling me you're gonna take your wife out, right?

ARNIE. It's Saturday night, she's been after me—

RAY. You just took her out—

ARNIE. Two weeks ago.

RAY. So what does she want? Some people you can't please.

ARNIE. Jesus, Ray, you know the situation, she's nervous—

RAY. I know, the electro-shock, I know. What I'm talking about is your commitment to what we're doing here. It's more than friendship, Arnie. You're a disciple. And you gotta be here for the meeting.

ARNIE. I've been here all day. I've been bowling with you, I've been drinking with you—

RAY. It's not the same thing. This is all we got left, we can't walk away from it. Call her and tell her you've gotta work tonight.

ARNIE. Is Phil absolutely coming?

RAY. He comes tonight or we're through with him. It's been weeks since I've even seen the son of a bitch.

ARNIE. I guess he's too good for us now. Big-time lawyer, house outta town.

RAY. He'll be here. He'll see I'm chosen. A lotta guys would like to be in your shoes, Arnie. The bottom falls out of every factory for fifty miles, people are begging in the streets, and this thing comes to me—

FAYE. (*Enters with a huge armful of wet laundry, which SHE drops on the floor.*) It's practically froze together.

RAY. The dryers were broke.

FAYE. All of 'em?

RAY. Except one. This kid was sending a dog around in it. The kid's smoking cigarettes and popping in quarters and the dog's going round and round. I waited a long time.

FAYE. You didn't say anything?

RAY. You know these kids, fifteen and they've done everything. He spooked me, looked like he'd already butchered a couple of his loved ones. You oughta be glad I'm alive.

FAYE. I'm delighted.

RAY. Maybe you could just iron 'em.

FAYE. You put 'em on and then maybe I'll iron 'em.

RAY. What's with the TV, anyway?

FAYE. We're selling it.

RAY. You just have to give it a little kick on the side and it's okay for a while.

FAYE. You want to eat something besides that Pilgrim filth? You want to pay the rent from two months back? There aren't anymore rooms to close off and it's still freezing in here—

RAY. Come on, not in front of Arnie.

(ARNIE is intently concentrating on the grease-stained newspaper.)

FAYE. Arnie knows the score. The TV's going tonight.

RAY. Yeah? Who'd buy that piece of junk?

FAYE. Some guy.

RAY. You got somebody? How'd you get somebody?

FAYE. I put an ad in the *Trader*. He called.

RAY. Listen to this, Arnie. *(To Faye.)* The vertical's out. The picture slides right off.

FAYE. He doesn't mind. He travels a lot.

RAY. You told him the vertical's out and he still wants it? How much?

FAYE. One hundred.

RAY. Nobody's gonna pay one hundred for that. Arnie, would you pay one hundred?

ARNIE. I already got a TV.

RAY. If you didn't.

ARNIE. I don't know. Seventy-five, anyway.

FAYE. See what I mean? *(SHE starts to unbutton her blouse.)* I'm gonna change.

RAY. How come you need to change to sell a damn TV?

(FAYE exits. ARNIE is still straining to read the newspaper.)

ARNIE. You see this, Ray? More lay-offs over in Lowell. The last plant shut down. What do you think?

RAY. Forget that, Arnie. All that is is news. Make your call and get the stuff so we can start when Phil gets here.

(ARNIE goes to the wall-phone.)

ARNIE. I'll tell her I had to work. She likes it when I'm at work.

RAY. You gotta call from the corner. They cut off our phone. Arnie, you gotta move quick. Soon as it gets dark, that pack of dogs starts moving. They been mixing it up with some youth gang from the projects. Sometimes at night you hear a scream and you can't tell if it's a dog or a kid. Soon as you get in the phone booth, pull the door shut. Use your head and they won't nail you.

ARNIE. I wish you'd get your damn phone hooked up again.

(ARNIE exits. RAY tries to read the paper. FAYE enters, wearing a very sexy dress.)

FAYE. Arnie leave?

RAY. What the hell are you looking like that for?

FAYE. You think I'm going out dressed like a Pilgrim?

RAY. Don't you get any more than seventy-five, you hear?

FAYE. He already said he'd pay one hundred.

RAY. He pays one hundred and I'll know what's going on. I'll see every goddam wrinkle in your dress.

FAYE. He's real interested in your car, too.

RAY. What does he know about my car?

FAYE. I mentioned it in the *Trader*.

RAY. That must have been one hell of an ad you wrote.

FAYE. I'll just show it to him, that's all.

RAY. I been with that car longer than I been with you, Faye. All the work I put into it when I could have been watching TV—so it shines like a jewel and always runs good. A lotta guys would like to own that car.

FAYE. Maybe he's one of 'em. I'll show it off. How much would you sell it for?

RAY. Christ, that would be like selling my best friend. *(Beat.)* I wouldn't take less than six grand.

FAYE. Okay.

RAY. What do you mean, "okay"?

FAYE. I mean he gives me six thousand dollars and the car is his. That's how you sell things.

RAY. How are you gonna get home if he buys the car?

FAYE. Oh, he'd have to give me a ride home if he buys the car, wouldn't he?

RAY. I don't like this.

FAYE. Six thousand bucks we're outta the woods for a spell. We don't need a car anymore. I can walk to work. *(FAYE puts her coat on.)*

RAY. I could go with you, Faye.

FAYE. I don't mind going alone.

RAY. You'd rather go alone?

FAYE. It'll be easier. I've talked to him, I can bargain him up.

RAY. You've never seen me in a card game.

FAYE. You really want to see how much you can get?

RAY. It has to be tonight?

FAYE. He's not gonna wait.

RAY. I got some guys coming by.

FAYE. So I'll take care of everything. Don't worry about it, Ray.

RAY. When you comin' back?

FAYE. Later on. First I gotta sell him the TV. Then he's gonna want to take a good long look at the car. How late are the boys staying? (*Beat.*) 'Cause I don't have to come straight back.

RAY. What are you gonna do, talk to *him*? I mean you don't even know him, right?

FAYE. Just from the *Trader*. I could go for a drink if you don't want me around.

RAY. Come back just as soon as you get his money, you hear?

FAYE. Would you get the TV?

RAY. (*Picks up the TV*) You think we'll ever get another one?

FAYE. Sure we will, Ray.

RAY. This here is just temporary, right?

FAYE. Oh, it's all temporary. Six thousand bucks we could even get color again. Take care of that laundry, would you?

RAY. I just wanna get you past the dogs.

(*RAY and FAYE exit, RAY carrying the TV. ARNIE climbs in the window from the fire escape. HE's carrying a duffel bag. HE takes a moment to catch his breath, then HE goes to the closet and gets out a trunk, which HE opens. HE gets a makeshift wooden altar from the trunk. RAY enters and puts the pile of laundry in the oven.*)

ARNIE. It's gettin' bad out there with the dogs.

RAY. Seems like there's more of 'em every day.

(RAY and ARNIE work together to set up the wooden altar. THEY put candles on it. ARNIE puts the full duffel bag next to the altar.)

ARNIE. I was out on the highway last night. There's always a lot after it rains.

RAY. Good work, Arnie. I bet we could sell the extras over at the Hungry Pilgrim. They can make seafood out of anything.

ARNIE. Now all we need is Phil.

(ARNIE reaches into the trunk and takes out a football helmet adorned with a TV antenna and Christmas lights. HE holds it a moment, then starts to put it on.)

RAY. Arnie! What are you doing?

ARNIE. Nothing, Ray. I just thought maybe I could give it a listen myself. Just for a minute—

RAY. You know better 'n that. It was me got chosen! I'm the only one that can hear.

ARNIE. I know that, Ray It's just ...

RAY. What, Arnie?

ARNIE. Sometimes I wish it was me got chosen.

RAY. I couldn't do this thing without you, Arnie. It coulda been you, really.

ARNIE. Yeah, it coulda been, but it wasn't. I knew it. I knew Phil wouldn't show. Now I got my wife falling all to pieces for nothing. If she's gonna crack up, it oughta be for a good reason—

RAY. They just did that touch-up work on her brain. She oughta be fine for a while.

ARNIE. You don't know, Ray. I gotta do something— she's got maps spread out all over the house. She says her problems aren't psychological, they're geographical.

RAY. What the hell does that mean?

ARNIE. It means she wants to move. I couldn't live without this, Ray. It's about all I got now.

(There's a sudden sharp KNOCKING at the door. It continues, urgently, right up until ARNIE opens the door. PHIL enters, shivering. HE is wearing a rumpled suit, no overcoat, and carrying a briefcase and a black leather bag.)

PHIL. Take your time, why don't you? It's freezing out there.

ARNIE. You oughta wear a coat.

PHIL. I lost my coat, okay? What is this, a trial?

(PHIL throws down his bags, sits down heavily and sighs. RAY and ARNIE exchange a look. Then RAY goes over to Phil.)

RAY. You lost your coat?

PHIL. I don't want to talk about it. I'm sitting on a park bench yesterday and it's warm, right? So I take off my coat, try to get a little sun. I guess I doze a little, 'cause the next thing I know, this son of a bitch dog has my coat in his teeth and he's running away. I chase him over a mile screaming at him to drop it. My whole body's pounding and aching and I just drop to my knees. And this dog turns to me with this look, like "C'mon, asshole. You giving up so soon?" There's my coat, jammed in his mouth and covered with dog-spit, so I figure, "Okay, you little bastard, you wanna play, I'll play, goddammit." So I sit there and he comes closer and closer and when he's about ten feet away, I spring through the air and he takes off and I chase that little fuck and he knows he's running for his life and I don't care about my coat—all I want is to kill this dog. I stop and pick up a brick and give it a heave, and damn if I don't hit him square in the back. I hear this yelping sound from deep in his throat and the last I see him he's headed up the entrance ramp on 95. Never even dropped the coat.

RAY. What are you doing in the park like that? You working part-time as a bum?

ARNIE. I figured you and me had that field covered, Ray.

PHIL. A bum? A bum? (*HE laughs without mirth.*) Listen, I'm onto something big. See that case? There's enough money in there to last the three of us the rest of our lives.

ARNIE. What'd you do, rob a bank?

RA.Y He's a lawyer, Arnie. He robs from everybody.

PHIL. Act right and maybe you guys get a piece of it.

ARNIE. I think he's serious.

RAY. Don't play with me, man. I haven't seen any money in six months.

PHIL. I'm not playing.

RAY. You mind if I take a look?

PHIL. Go on.

ARNIE. You're really talking millions of bucks?

PHIL. You heard me.

RAY. (*To Arnie.*) He's just holding it for somebody, I bet. (*RAY opens the case.*) What is this shit? (*HE holds up a spray can.*)

PHIL. That's money, just like I said. The stuff is incredible. Your house smells like a barn. No problem, just give it a spray and it's like a new house—(*HE sprays the room. Then HE grabs another spray can from the case.*) Maybe you spill something, right? (*HE kicks over a beer.*) There won't be a stain with this—(*HE sprays the rug.*)

RAY. Shit, man. There prob'ly won't be a rug, either!

PHIL. (*Grabs scissors from the case.*) Gimme a penny! Hurry up, you're not gonna believe this—Arnie, I'm talking to you—

(*ARNIE tosses him a penny.*)

PHIL. These'll cut through it like it's Swiss fucking cheese! (*PHIL struggles to cut the penny, then tosses it aside.*) Damn! It usually works. The point is, these are the best scissors ever made.

ARNIE. So?

RAY. What's with you, Phil?

ARNIE. Where's the money?

PHIL. All this stuff is money, as soon as we sell it.

RAY. Sell it? You're selling this stuff?

PHIL. Hey, I'm really sorry I tried to help you guys out. Arnie, stacking up cat-food at the 7-Eleven, Ray, slinking around the house like a wounded animal—

ARNIE. You know this racket, Ray? He signs us up and makes bucks off what we sell.

RAY. Kind of a blood-sucker arrangement, right?

PHIL. Yeah, but then you sign up other salesmen—

ARNIE. And *they* sign up other salesmen—

RAY. 'Til everybody's rushing door to door selling Amway, but nobody's home 'cause they're selling Amway.

ARNIE. What's goin' on, Phil?

RAY. They bounce you outta that fancy law firm?

PHIL. Forget it.

ARNIE. You're headed for the top with that degree of yours. It's me and Ray that are paying the price.

PHIL. Look, I'm not exactly a lawyer anymore. I sort of got disbarred.

RAY. First your coat, now this.

ARNIE. So what happened?

PHIL. Just a simple misunderstanding. I'm not s'posed to talk about it.

RAY. We're your friends, Phil.

ARNIE. Prob'ly your only friends.

PHIL. Well ... someone made some careless errors filing some wills. Our whole firm is under investigation.

RAY. Did they find who did it?

PHIL. The problem was that monies were apparently misdirected into funds controlled by myself. I will have no further comment.

RAY. That don't sound good.

ARNIE. You couldn't join another firm?

PHIL. Other firms won't take graduates of my school.

ARNIE. What was your school, anyway?

PHIL. That's not the point. The point is, I paid damn good money for that degree and now I find out it's only good at this one firm. They sure didn't tell me that when I bought it.

RAY. Sounds like you got ripped off.

PHIL. Damn straight. I'm considering legal action as soon as this thing blows over.

ARNIE. Well, I sure am sorry to hear that, Phil.

PHIL. Sorry? You're sorry? Gimme a break, Arnie, this is the best thing that ever happened to me. I'm a natural salesman. That's what I shoulda been all along.

ARNIE. Yeah, sure. You're a natural. Isn't he a natural, Ray?

PHIL. You take a good salesman and a good product and we're talking serious dollars. And hell, it's not even work, it's talking to people, just like I'm talking to you. So, can I sign you up? mean, I got about a million other people I could go to, but I figured I'd give you guys first shot. Old times sake and all—

CRYSTAL. (*Enters from outside.*) You sure this is the right house, Phil?

PHIL. Honey? I thought I told you to wait in the car.

RAY. (*To Arnie.*) "Honey?"

CRYSTAL. I am sick to death of the car. It's been a month, Phil. You promised you'd find us a real place to stay. I hate lying around that car with all your samples.

PHIL. I understand exactly how you feel. Maybe we could talk about this later.

CRYSTAL. You just want to be in a house. I'm not staying in the car while you're in a house.

PHIL. You're absolutely right, darling. (*HE turns to Ray and Arnie.*) Ray, Arnie ... I want you to meet the new love of my life. Crystal, honey, these are the best friends a guy could ever want.

CRYSTAL. It's really nice to meet you.

PHIL. The thing is, there are some things I want to talk about with my life-long friends.

CRYSTAL. Go on, I don't care. (*To Ray.*) You live here? You got anything to get me off? I'm feeling pretty earth-bound tonight.

PHIL. You don't need anything.

CRYSTAL. You're so straight it's dangerous.

RAY. You want a beer?

CRYSTAL. A beer? They still make that stuff? (*CRYSTAL rummages through the case.*)

PHIL. Please, honey. Those are my samples.

CRYSTAL. I got a buzz off the oven cleaner once, remember? Real pretty, but hell coming down.

PHIL. Hey! I need that!

CRYSTAL. (*Taking the can.*) This oughta get the job done. Isn't that what you tell the customers?

PHIL. As long as you're taking it, maybe you'd like to go out to the car.

CRYSTAL. I didn't get out of the car just to get right back in. (*To Ray.*) He hates seeing me get off. He thinks I got a heart of gold, but he's wrong.

PHIL. Is the other room okay?

RAY. Just perfect. I love dope addicts crawling around my house.

(*PHIL leads CRYSTAL into the other room.*)

ARNIE. She even makes his wife look good.

RAY. Now we can get this thing going.

ARNIE. You gotta hear that voice again, Ray. That one time wasn't enough.

RAY. I'll give it my best shot. That's all I can do.

ARNIE. I just gotta know it's really there.

PHIL. (*Returns from the den.*) What's going on? There's no furniture in there.

RAY. Me and Faye burned it. You see what they charge for firewood now?

ARNIE. She's really getting off on the cleaner, Phil?

PHIL. Give her a break, it's just a stage she's going through.

RAY. So that's what you been doing, Phil. Living in the fast lane.

ARNIE. Sounds to me like he's living in his car.

PHIL. I just wish I'd met her ten years ago.

ARNIE. Oh, you mean when she was nine?

PHIL. God, it's been wonderful, she's really opened my eyes. I guess I never thought sex could be so ... dirty.

ARNIE. You're married, Phil.

PHIL. I'm happy, goddammit! Isn't that good enough for you guys?

RAY. What'd you bring her for? This is our thing, Phil.

ARNIE. He didn't bring her, Ray. She lives right out there. She lives wherever Phil parks the car.

RAY. Well you ruined everything. We got the full moon, Faye's outta the house, and you show up with this creature—

PHIL. She won't bother us. Unless you want her to.

RAY. What do you mean?

PHIL. Join this thing—whatever it is.

ARNIE. Yeah? You think she'd do it?

PHIL. I haven't been able to think of one thing she won't do. And don't think I haven't tried.

RAY. Forget it, Phil. You just oughta be glad me and Arnie asked you to join.

ARNIE. Ray? If we got the truth, then maybe we oughta let others in on it too.

PHIL. What's going on, anyway? Arnie tells me you got on the roof and you heard something—

RAY. That's right. And the time will come when I hear it again. We gotta be ready.

ARNIE. It's gonna change your life, Phil. There's something out there. It talked to Ray.

RAY. If you don't want in, well, you can pack up your date and get outta here, Phil. Because me and Arnie have gotta get started.

PHIL. I'll give it a try, long as it don't cost money. (*Beat.*) And maybe in return, you guys re-think Amway. One hand washes the other, you know what I'm saying?

RAY. You bring the ritual feast like I asked?

PHIL. (*Opens his briefcase.*) Everybody like pepperoni?

ARNIE. Suits me.

PHIL. Louie's was the only place open. (*Takes the pizza out of the briefcase and places it by the altar. To Ray.*) So what'd the Big Guy tell you, anyway?

RAY. Bits and pieces. It was really there, Phil, right up there on the roof, a voice talking to me. Telling me to hold on because the factory's opening up again.

PHIL. And nothing since?

ARNIE. He tries real hard.

RAY. But I feel it, right in this house, I feel it all around me. I never won a goddam thing in my life and I get picked out of everybody in the whole world. It almost makes you think.

PHIL. I'm gonna talk straight to you, Ray. I've known you my whole life, so I know you're not lying. But the fact is, you're only as good as your product. Right now you got nothing to sell.

ARNIE. Just maybe we got salvation, Phil.

PHIL. Sure, sure, but without money, big deal. You know what I'm saying? We gotta rope in people who will turn over their life savings. We need a community of followers to get out and sell this thing. I don't know what it's gonna take, but the fact is right now we are just three guys in a cold house with a pizza.

ARNIE. You hear this, Ray? He's going Amway on us.

RAY. The one true way does not mean money, Phil. It's about something better.

PHIL. Better than money?

RAY. That's right.

PHIL. Then you oughta let other people in on it, right?

RAY. That's just what I'm doing.

PHIL. How many people you got?

RAY. Well ... Arnie here, for starters.

PHIL. With all due respect, Ray, I am telling you I smell dollars. But the competition out there is tough.

RAY. But I'm the real thing.

PHIL. Exactly. The direct link-up. You and this voice. No middle-man. That's value you're just not going to find anywhere else. True value. The True Value Church! What do you think?

RAY. I think we better get started before Faye shows up.

ARNIE. We could live with that, Ray. The True Value Church.

PHIL. Marketing is the key, just like anything. You take a look at the guys that went big-time from Jesus on down, they got packaged right and the rest is history, as they say. Let's go public, get you some exposure, put you on TV, let the people out there know they gotta move fast and get on the band-wagon—

RAY. Only if it helps me spread the word.

PHIL. It absolutely will. And the dollars will be there.

RAY. Maybe tonight we turn it around. Gimme the helmet, Arnie. The True Value Church is now in session.

PHIL. What am I s'posed to do?

RAY. Take off your shirt and do like Arnie does. Everything got told to me that night. We keep doing it and it's gonna happen for us.

(RAY, ARNIE, and PHIL strip off their shirts. ARNIE gets the helmet from the trunk and hands it to RAY, who solemnly places it on his head. ARNIE places the duffel bag up on the altar, then turns down the lights. RAY stands by the altar with the flickering candles and PHIL and ARNIE crouch in front of him. RAY turns on the blinking Christmas tree lights on the helmet.)

PHIL. This is what the voice told you?

ARNIE. Would you shut up?

(RAY takes a bite of pizza and hands it to PHIL and ARNIE, who also bite into it. CRYSTAL wanders in, drugged, from the other room. THEY don't see her.)

RAY. I feel the power ... it's coming down outta the sky ... right through the miles of blackness and the clouds from some higher place and we're pulling it down into this room ... something in the air is changing ... it's casting a spell and nobody here is ever gonna be the same again. I'm feeling it stronger and stronger and now I'm gonna hear the voice ...

(A pause as RAY concentrates. Then CRYSTAL screams and falls to the floor.)

RAY. Where did she come from?

(ARNIE turns on the lights. CRYSTAL is lying on the floor, very still. PHIL rushes to her.)

PHIL. Hey, it's me, baby. Wake up.
ARNIE. You think it was a sign from above?
PHIL. That or an overdose.
RAY. I knew she was a mistake. Get her out of here.

(PHIL carries Crystal out the door, then comes right back. SOUNDS from outside.)

PHIL. Somebody's coming up the stairs!
RAY. Let's get this stuff outta here.
PHIL. What about her?
RAY. Move her!
PHIL. The basement?
RAY. She'll freeze down there. Take her to the bedroom.

(PHIL and ARNIE carry Crystal from the room. A single candle is burning. BILL, a large, man in a dark blue suit, bursts into the room. FAYE enters and sees BILL and RAY staring at each other, Ray shirtless.)

RAY. (*To Faye.*) You might as well know, I been chosen.

FAYE. Chosen what?

RAY. I been chosen. Chosen.

FAYE. It's gotta be better than unemployment. (*Beat.*) Ray? This here is Bill.

RAY. I guess you must have bought my car, Bill.

BILL. Sure didn't.

RAY. That's the only reason you could have drove my wife home is if you bought the car.

FAYE. He was *thinking* of buying it. What he bought was the TV.

RAY. How much?

FAYE. One twenty-five.

RAY. I told you to stay under one hundred.

(BILL goes to the refrigerator and gets a beer. RAY puts on his shirt.)

BILL. That's right. One twenty-five.

RAY. Wasn't worth it. You can have it for seventy-five.

BILL. I already paid.

RAY. I won't let it go for that. You pay more than seventy-five it's no sale.

BILL. I'll come down to one-fifteen. That's as low as I'll go.

RAY. I'll come up to one hundred. How's that?

BILL. Forget it. No way I go down to one hundred. I paid one twenty-five and that's final.

RAY. I'm telling you it's not worth it!

BILL. (*To Faye.*) I don't know. You think it was worth it?

RAY. Where the hell is my car if you got a ride?

FAYE. We had some problems.

BILL. Took a little test drive, Ray. The damn thing died on us.

RAY. I had it running perfect. It wouldn't have just died like that.

FAYE. Actually, it wouldn't start is what happened.

RAY. So it's at your house.

BILL. Don't talk houses to me. I'll break your fucking neck.

FAYE. We took it for a test drive like Bill said. And it wouldn't start up again.

RAY. Why'd you shut if off then, huh? If you were test-driving it, why'd you have to stop?

BILL. What is this, some kind of a half-assed court of law?

RAY. I want my car.

BILL. It's out by the quarry. A little off the road. Nice quiet spot overlooking the water.

RAY. How come you took it out there?

BILL. You ever been out to the quarry, Ray?

RAY. You live here your whole life it's something you do.

BILL. Ain't it something when the moon's full? And it kind of glistens off the water?

RAY. Sure, we'd take girls out there in the summer, go skinny-dipping, the whole thing. A coupla six-packs, hell, anything can happen.

(RAY and BILL laugh. Pause.)

RAY. I guess you just wanted to see the quarry, right?

BILL. That's right. Check it out. Give it the once-over. Damn shame about your car.

FAYE. Bill wanted to see how it handled the bad roads. He turned it off and later it wouldn't start.

RAY. Looks like you'll have to get it towed outta there, Bill.

BILL. Let it rot.

RAY. What was that?

BILL. Let the fucking thing rot. It's not my car.

RAY. Well, Jesus, *I'm* not about to tow it out. I didn't do a crazy-ass thing like take it to the quarry in the middle of winter. It's against the law even being out there now. A lotta dope changes hands and they're cracking down.

BILL. Oh, all kinds of shit goes down out there. Me and Faye saw some people—what the hell were they doing?

FAYE. I don't know. Chasing somebody. Ganging up on him, or maybe it was just some kind of game.

BILL. (*Laughs.*) That's what it was. Some kind of game.

RAY. I'll be straight with you, Bill. No way do I pull my car outta there.

BILL. Well, that could be a problem, Ray. I figure they'll get you one way or the other.

RAY. Who's gonna get me?

BILL. They got these garages where they break the cars down and build new ones from all the parts. These bastards work quick—a couple of hours your car don't even exist no more. It's part of ten other cars that could drive by and you wouldn't even know it.

RAY. You seem to know the field pretty good.

BILL. What's worse is if the cops get there first. They stick a little smack under the seat, trace the plates, then plant your ass in Walpole State Prison for ten years. I'd say your future's looking mighty bleak.

RAY. Why'd you go out there if you know all that?

BILL. You got any scotch?

FAYE. Over the sink.

(BILL gets the scotch.)

RAY. I bet I could get it started.

BILL. The car is dead. No way you'll ever get it going again.

RAY. What am I s'posed to do?

FAYE. Tell him, Bill. Bill had an idea.

BILL. The way I figure it, Ray, you're down to one option. Take my pick-up out there. In the back you find a can of gasoline. That and a match oughta rectify this little dilemma.

RAY. What kind of a shit-heel idea is that?

FAYE. We'd get the insurance money. We report the car is missing and they have to pay us. If it just sits there, well—

BILL. It's Walpole for you, baby. Ten years of solitude with only violent sex attacks to break the monotony.

FAYE. This is just like selling it, almost. They find the burned-up car, we get our money.

RAY. I've had that car since I was eighteen.

BILL. Stop dreaming. You'll never drive it again. Get out there like a man and cut your losses. Burn the car and be done with it.

FAYE. How are we gonna sleep, waiting for that knock on the door?

BILL. They drag you out in the night—work you over with screwdrivers and cigarette lighters 'til you confess—

RAY. I didn't do anything!

BILL. Everybody's guilty. Some people manage to beat the rap, that's all.

FAYE. Do it for us, Ray. There's not much more furniture to burn. Think about what we could do with that insurance money—

BILL. Soak it down real good. Then make yourself some kind of a fuse. Light that sucker and get behind a rock or something. It's Christmas morning times ten when it blows. Then you're home free. (*BILL gets out some money.*) Here you go. Expense money.

RAY. We'll deduct that from the TV to bring you under one hundred.

BILL. I paid one twenty-five for the TV! It's expense money or you don't get it! (*BILL goes to the counter and starts eating the fried clams.*)

RAY. I gotta do it, don't I?

FAYE. It would make me so proud. I bet it would take us right through to spring. It's almost like a job, you know?

(*BILL tosses the keys to the pick-up to Ray.*)

FAYE. Take care of yourself, Ray. And dress warm, there's a hard wind blowing out there tonight.

RAY. I'll be okay. It's just one of those things I gotta do.

BILL. You'll do fine, Ray. You're a natural, I can tell just by looking.

(RAY puts on his coat and exits.)

BILL. What kind of lousy decor is this, huh?

FAYE. He must have been working on something.

BILL. Your husband, I don't know, he must think he's some kind of a big deal, living in a house. I never lived in no house. He ever mentions it again I'll rip him apart with my bare hands.

FAYE. He didn't mean anything by it. It was just talk.

(BILL has been pacing. Now HE finds the pizza in Phil's briefcase. PHIL enters from the other room. HE puts on his shirt.)

PHIL. Hello, Faye.

FAYE. Phil! Didn't even know you were here. It's been ages.

PHIL. Oh, I've been busy.

FAYE. *(To Bill.)* Phil is a lawyer.

BILL. Lawyers are parasites. They'd suck the puss out of an open wound if they thought there was a coin inside.

PHIL. Actually, I'm disbarred, if it makes a difference.

FAYE. *(To Phil.)* This is Bill.

PHIL. Hello, Bill.

(BILL opens the briefcase and takes out a slice of pizza.)

PHIL. Hey! Hold it right there, Mister. *(Beat.)* That pizza's for us. I bought it myself.

BILL. Scroungy bastard. You couldn't spare a slice?

PHIL. It's not really pizza. I mean, it's not *just* pizza I think it's actually kind of an offering, but don't quote me. (*Beat.*) Look, I've been under a lot of stress lately. I'm not living with my wife anymore.

FAYE. You were in my bedroom, weren't you?

PHIL. I guess I was.

FAYE. Alone?

PHIL. To the best of my knowledge yes. Alone.

(ARNIE enters from the other room. HE also puts on his shirt.)

ARNIE. Thought you were getting her a glass of water, Phil.

PHIL. (*To Faye.*) Arnie is here too. (*To Arnie.*) This guy is about to eat the ritual feast.

ARNIE. I'll be damned. (*To Bill.*) Don't mess with that stuff. It's not what you think.

(BILL closely examines the pizza.)

FAYE. His name is Bill.

BILL. Generous bunch of bastards.

ARNIE. It would be different if it was just pizza, but it isn't. We need it for a higher purpose. (*ARNIE comes over to Bill.*) So ... new in town?

(BILL glares at him.)

ARNIE. We don't get many new neighbors. Sometimes the mental hospital unloads a houseful, but that's about it. *(To Faye.)* Where's Ray?

FAYE. He had to leave for a while.

BILL. He went out to the quarry to torch his car.

ARNIE. He can't be leaving right in the middle of it like that!

BILL. *(Laughs.)* I bet they were in the middle of something.

FAYE. What do you guys do in here, anyway? What's that all about?

PHIL. It's nothing.

BILL. Three of 'em, sitting in the dark with the door closed. Pretending they're drunker than they really are, so they don't have to notice the hands creeping all over each other. Hearts pounding like jack-hammers. Breathing so loud it wakes the neighbors. Something different, some dirty little thrills. Afterwards, staring at the floor, acting like it never happened. Look at 'em.

ARNIE. It's not like that.

BILL. The hell it isn't. *(HE picks up the pizza slice.)*

ARNIE. I'm warning you—

PHIL. Put it down, you son of a bitch!

(BILL slowly raises the pizza to his mouth and takes a large bite. CRYSTAL wanders in from the other room.)

CRYSTAL. Phil? Let's get outta here, Phil. Some kind of spirits were coming down from the sky and you were there, Phil. You were one of the ones ... *(To Arnie.)* And you, too. And the other guy. Casting some kind of a spell, and then it all went black—

PHIL. That was just a dream, Crystal.

CRYSTAL. I been having such weird dreams lately.

FAYE. What's going on here?

BILL. A goddam supernatural circle-jerk, right in the family room.

FAYE. Who is she?

PHIL. She's with me.

BILL. Oh, the Big Brother Program. Helping young girls through the rocky waters of adolescence. You oughta be honored for service to the community.

CRYSTAL. Wait! It wasn't a dream, was it! It was real. (*CRYSTAL crosses to the altar where the duffel bag is. SHE looks in.*) I knew it!

ARNIE. Stay outta there!

BILL. (*Looks in bag.*) Some kind of a franchise you're running. Transforming taxpayers into dead house pets. (*To Faye.*) Quite a harvest. Maybe these are the neighbors—the ones that used to live in all them boarded up houses. Maybe it's gonna be us.

FAYE. I thought I knew you guys.

ARNIE. We found something, Faye. Something powerful. Something worth bowing down to.

BILL. Yeah? What'd you find, little man?

PHIL. It's nothing, really—

ARNIE. I'm not gonna talk about it.

BILL. I think you'll talk about it.

PHIL. Who are you, anyway?

BILL. My organization is going to be very active in your community. It's up to me to scout things out so things run smoothly. You know what I'm saying?

PHIL. Oh, a trouble-shooter.

BILL. That's right. I'm a trouble-shooter. I'll be honest. I don't like what I see in your town. I want things to go smooth and what do I find but a pack of half-drunk devil worshipers carrying on.

PHIL. I'm not really involved. I was just observing.

BILL. We're gonna keep tabs on you, for the good of the community. I'll need your addresses.

ARNIE. I'm not saying a word until I talk to my lawyer.

BILL. (*Grabs Arnie by the neck and forces him to the floor.*) Who's your lawyer?

ARNIE. Him.

PHIL. Give him your address, Arnie.

ARNIE. 326 Bullfinch, here in town.

BILL. (*Releases Arnie and turns menacingly on Phil.*) How about you?

PHIL. 273-ADQ.

BILL. What the hell is that?

PHIL. My license plate. I live in my car. With her. Look, do you want to hear how you can make a whole pile of money just talking to people the way we're talking right now?

BILL. I know how to make money. I practically invented money. So don't waste my time. (*Advancing on Arnie.*) True believers cause problems in the business world. How'd you get into this?

ARNIE. Ray oughta tell you.

BILL. Ray ain't here.

FAYE. You better tell him, Arnie. He's excitable if he doesn't get what he wants.

BILL. That's just what I am, Tinkerbell. I'm excitable.

ARNIE. Well ... after the plant closed down I got my career going over at the 7-Eleven and Phil bought the degree. But Ray, you remember, Faye, all he did was watch TV.

FAYE. All the time—

ARNIE. He kept watching and watching and moving closer to the set and it was all he had, you know? And he wasn't even sleeping, just staring at the TV day and night, but you know how Ray is. After a while just watching TV wasn't enough anymore. He had to become the TV. So he strapped the antenna to his head and crawled up on the roof one night and he's standing there bare-assed on the roof, gulping down whiskey with the rain coming down all around him and the lightning flashing and he hears a voice telling him that the plant was going to open and what to do to hold on to his life. So he done it the best he could, with the animals and the pizza. And now he's just waiting for a sign. He clued me in, Phil came up with the name, and that's how the True Value Church got started.

FAYE. God, I wish he'd just get a job like anybody else.

ARNIE. What Ray has got is better than any goddam job. He's got the truth living inside him.

RAY. (*Enters in a state of great excitement. HE tosses an empty gas can to the corner and rips off his coat.*) Oh, lord, it was the best thing I ever saw! There it was, all peaceful by the water. I get in, turn on the radio full-blast, then soak the thing down real good. I'm hiding back of a rock as the fuse burns down and pretty soon the whole thing goes, just a big beautiful blast. In the light of the flames I see these other faces come out of the dark, watching. When it burns down a bit, some of 'em come forward and give it a push and it rolls down the bank and hits the water still burning with the radio blasting while it goes under. We all stood there, me and these people, pulled together by the flames. The new age is coming right outta them flames, and it started tonight, burning up the old and building the new. I looked at all them faces staring at the fire and I saw 'em for what they are—true believers! I tell you, boys, we're on our way.

BILL. You do good work, Ray.

RAY. I couldn't have done it if it weren't for you. You been sent to us for a purpose. I know you have, Bill.

(BILL comes up behind Ray, collars him, and forces him down into a straight chair. HE takes a lamp and twists it so it's shining in Ray's face. The LIGHTS in the room fade out, and RAY stares into the glare of the lamp as if under interrogation.)

BILL. You're right on the money, Ray. I come here for a purpose. Now I got some questions for you.

(The rising sound of the pack of DOGS outside.)

BLACKOUT

END OF ACT I

ACT II

(Morning, several days later. LIGHTS up on the room.
More of the furniture has been burned.

BILL enters from outside. HE takes off his overcoat,
throws it over a chair, and opens his briefcase. HE's
going through papers when FAYE enters in her
bathrobe.)

FAYE. I thought you were Ray.

BILL. I ain't Ray.

FAYE. I wanted him to put another chair on the fire.

BILL. They said snow. It's nothing but a cold rain out
there.

FAYE. Where is he, anyway?

BILL. Still working.

FAYE. All night?

BILL. I worked all night! Why shouldn't he?

FAYE. I'm the only one that sleeps around here
anymore.

BILL. There's a lot that needs getting done. And we're
doin' it.

FAYE. *(Goes to the kitchen and pours coffee for both*
of them.) God I wish I was someplace warm.

BILL. Stick around. Things are heating up right here in
town.

FAYE. I plan to stick around. Last night they made me
manager over at the Pilgrim. I been there three and a half
weeks so I got seniority over everybody. I get to divide up

41

the tips myself—anybody looks at me wrong I can just fire
'em. (*SHE starts for the hall.*) You tell Ray to put
something on the fire when he gets in. I gotta get ready for
work. (*FAYE exits.*)

(*BILL gets out a clipboard from his briefcase and starts
doing some quick calculations. CRYSTAL enters from
outside. SHE's wearing one of PHIL's tee-shirts as a
nightgown and is carrying a toothbrush.*)

CRYSTAL. Morning, Bill.
BILL. It must be freezing in that garage. Why don't you
sleep inside like people?
CRYSTAL. Phil has too much pride. The car isn't so
bad. We got it fixed up just the way we like it.
BILL. (*Goes to her and touches her hair, very gently.*)
People die like that. They wake up in the backseat, three
A.M. and the cold has sunk itself right into their bones. So
they turn on the heater and they start to warm up and all
the while the fumes are taking over, easing the life out of
'em as gentle as a first kiss. Let's you and me take another
drive like the last one. Under them trees we're a million
miles from all this.
CRYSTAL. (*Pulling away.*) I can't. Phil's off
delivering Home Care products. I'm s'posed to clean the
garage. Then my rehab group is taking some orphans on a
field trip to Lowell.
BILL. You got your whole goddam life planned, don't
you?
CRYSTAL. Phil's gonna need a new job. That's the
only reason I went with you, Bill.

BILL. Yeah, well, maybe that wasn't enough. Maybe it'll take another trip out to the quarry before anything comes through.

CRYSTAL. You shouldn't hit on me like this. I had a bad childhood.

BILL. Who didn't? You think about it, Crystal. Somebody's bound to take care of Phil if he keeps pushing that Amway on people.

(CRYSTAL exits to bathroom. BILL rips apart a straight chair for firewood. RAY enters from outside, carrying a gas can.)

BILL. How'd it go last night?

RAY. You shoulda seen us, man. Me and Arnie took 'em out one after the other, up one side of the street and down the other. Check the list, check the plates, douse it, light it, move on down the line. Teamwork, just like playing ball. I swear I can burn cars in my sleep now.

BILL. You learn a lot in two days.

RAY. There was two Hondas on North Street. We hit 'em both.

BILL. *(Checks the list.)* I can only pay you for one.

RAY. We couldn't tell! The first one didn't have no plates!

BILL. Get real, Ray, this ain't a charity. I can't pay you if I don't get paid. The owner didn't order his car burned then I don't see any money. This is the real world.

RAY. Shit. Me and Arnie were counting on that first Honda! We had the bucks all figured out.

BILL. *(Opens his briefcase and takes out a stack of money.)* This here is all yours, Ray. You're doing a helluva job.

RAY. Thanks.

(RAY reaches for the money, but BILL is already returning it to the briefcase, which HE snaps shut. HE gets out a voucher and hands it to Ray.)

BILL. Here's your voucher.

RAY. What's this? No money?

BILL. That's a lot safer than carrying money. Cash it in and you're gonna be a wealthy man. We got back orders comin' in all night long. The phone in the office is ringing off the hook with people needing their cars torched. There's no time to sleep. And that ain't all. I talked to my people last night and there are good residential possibilities.

RAY. Here in town?

BILL. The south side. It's building by building for now, but we may get a whole block. The money is there, the commitment is there, now it's in the hands of the lawyers.

RAY. Which block?

BILL. South, Bullfinch, and Applegate Lane. The building that's definitely going is 326 Bullfinch. Three-decker.

RAY. That's where Arnie lives.

BILL. I deal with landlords, Ray. It's upward mobility, the fast-track. You're one lucky son of a bitch.

RAY. I'm s'posed to burn down my best friend's house?

BILL. You'd rather have a stranger do it? Someone who doesn't care and makes a mess of it? I think you owe this to your friend. It's getting burned anyway.

RAY. I better tell Arnie. Maybe he can get his things out.

BILL. Where is he?

RAY. I dropped him at the mall to hand out leaflets for the church. Tonight we do it, Bill. Tonight we're gonna put the True Value Church out on the street. Phil's got a marketing plan and we're going to the people.

BILL. Listen to me, Ray, as soon as I met you, I saw the potential. A guy like you tuned into another frequency is perfect for the arson business. The flames get inside your head and you gotta have more. But now you gotta choose. I need a commitment. You either get in line with my people and make something of yourself or spin off into your own sick little dream world. You can't do both, you gotta choose.

RAY. You're asking me to give up my church?

BILL. Or else you're out in the cold. I'm the only game in town.

RAY. This is my life. I gotta think it through.

BILL. (*Picks up the chair he destroyed.*) I gotta make some calls. (*HE starts for the door.*) Can I count you in?

RAY. I gotta talk it out with Faye.

BILL. Jesus Christ, you don't even know what I'm offering, do you? Most guys put in three to five *years* with cars before they get offered a building. Here, you do two *days* with cars, you get offered a building and you fumble the ball. There's a lotta free agents out there, Ray. A lotta guys played out their options that are aching for an opportunity like this. All you gotta do is choose right and you're home free. That's all I'm gonna say. (*BILL exits.*)

(*RAY gets a cup of coffee. CRYSTAL comes back from the bathroom. She's changed into jeans and a sweater.*)

CRYSTAL. Hi, Ray.

RAY. You guys doing okay out there?

CRYSTAL. It's fine. It's the longest I ever lived in one place.

RAY. You can stay inside if you want.

CRYSTAL. I like it better out there. We took the back seat out and put up some curtains and it really feels like home. Phil found a birdbath on somebody's lawn and it looks real nice next to the car.

RAY. He must have left early this morning.

CRYSTAL. He had some deliveries. (*SHE comes closer to Ray.*) Ray? He's been real nervous lately. The middle of the night he can't sleep so he climbs up to the front seat and drives off. I wake up in a strange driveway. And Phil's up there banging on somebody's door, trying to get 'em to buy. Who's going to buy floor wax at two in the morning? He yells at them, tells 'em they should be ashamed of their house. I get scared he might do something—

RAY. That high pressure stuff don't work. I'll talk to him, okay?

CRYSTAL. Thanks, Ray. And thanks for helping me get straight.

RAY. What'd I do?

CRYSTAL. That spell you cast? I been different ever since. I got right into rehab.

RAY. Yeah? I did that for you?

CRYSTAL. It's a powerful thing you got, Ray. We'd like to have you and Faye down to our place for a visit sometime. (*CRYSTAL exits to the garage.*)

FAYE. (*Enters in her Pilgrim outfit.*) I was starting to think you'd never come home.

RAY. The work just keeps piling up. Now it looks like I'm getting a promotion. If I want it.

FAYE. You too? They made me manager last night.

RAY. That's great, Faye. You earned it, all the time you put in.

FAYE. Almost a month. It gets me thinking maybe we got some kind of hope after all.

RAY. We always had hope. But now we got money to go with it. (*RAY kisses Faye*) How would you feel if we burned down Arnie's house?

FAYE. I think you should talk to Arnie. I really don't know the business, Ray.

RAY. Bill says it's a real break for me.

FAYE. Then maybe you better do it. It's been a long time since we had any real breaks.

RAY. We got anything to eat?

FAYE. I stole some chowder last night. And that pizza of yours is still underfoot. (*FAYE starts trying to clean up the clutter in the room.*)

RAY. Don't be touching the pizza! And stay away from them animals, too!

FAYE. It's making me crazy, Ray, all the stuff you bring into our home.

RAY. Live with it a little longer, Faye. It's gonna be worth it in the end.

FAYE. What you need is a good night's sleep. It's been three straight days of this.

(PHIL bursts in from the garage. He's wearing an overcoat. HE glares at Ray and Faye.)

RAY. Hey, buddy. I gotta talk to you. Crystal says you're working too hard. I'm thinking, you lighten up the approach, maybe try to catch people when they're awake, it might help sales.

PHIL. You're telling me how to sell? You get a goddam job and now you know how to do my job too? Huh?

RAY. Phil, I'm not saying that—

PHIL. They don't buy. They say they'll think it over, I go back and they still won't buy. Or maybe they order and they don't pay. Sometimes I knock and they won't even come to the door. I see 'em in there staring at the TV and they won't even get up.

RAY. It's tough work, busting in cold on strangers like that.

PHIL. Strangers? Listen, my own wife—I swallowed my last ounce of pride and knocked on her door. She looked at all the samples and she said she'd let me know if she needed anything. The house was a mess, she needs everything I got. But she wouldn't order a goddam thing—

RAY. It takes time—

PHIL. That was my own house I was going into! My house and my wife and she wouldn't order a thing! I think she even stole some of the stuff. And then I gotta go out to the car and tell Crystal I couldn't even make a sale to my own wife. How do you think that makes me feel?

RAY. I think maybe you're trying too hard.

PHIL. There's no bucks in the Church. You got nobody but me and Arnie.

RAY. Don't talk like that, Phil. It's the one true way.

PHIL. It's been three goddam days, I mean, how long are we s'posed to wait? If the Church won't fly then all I got left is Amway.

RAY. Arnie's out at the mall, just like you suggested. We're rounding up followers.

PHIL. You call yourself a man of God and you never even been on television—

RAY. All I'm askin' for is time. Whatever it is, it's in this house, Phil. I just have to hear it—

PHIL. I got a gun in my pocket. I'm settling all my accounts today. The first thing I'm doing is putting you guys down for some orders. Now what do you want?

RAY. What do you mean?

PHIL. (*On the verge of tears.*) I mean I know you for twenty-five years and you won't even buy a bottle of goddam window-cleaner. I plan to change that. (*PHIL takes the pistol out and puts it on the table.*)

RAY. This is just what I'm talking about with the high pressure stuff. It don't work.

PHIL. No? Well sales is my turf, Ray, and I say it works. (*HE puts his hand on the gun.*) What do you need, Faye? (*PHIL picks up the gun. His hands are trembling.*) I'm talking to you, Faye, and I want an answer.

FAYE. Well ... I guess we could use ...

RAY. You sell shoe polish, Phil?

(*PHIL nods.*)

FAYE. We'll take some. And some, uh, oven cleaner.

PHIL. See? It works, Ray. So don't tell me what works ever again. By the end of the day, I'm gonna get a lot more orders. I'm gonna get enough so I win the trip to France. You think about that while you're cleaning your goddam oven. France.

RAY. Good luck.

PHIL. Sales isn't luck, it's attitude ... you gotta have a can-do attitude. Clients pick up on that the minute you walk in. Attitude.

FAYE. You're doing real good so far, Phil.

PHIL. You're buying this stuff 'cause you need it, right? Because if I thought you were buying it out of pity, I wouldn't sell it to you. I'd prob'ly shoot you, you understand me?

FAYE. We need it, Phil.

PHIL. You're goddam right you need it. I been poking around in here. You need a lot. See, I'm just trying to help out. (*Starts writing down the orders.*)

CRYSTAL. (*Comes in with her coat on.*) Phil? It's time for my field trip. I don't wanna keep the orphans waiting. (*SHE sees Phil recording the orders.*) Oh, he made you buy.

PHIL. I didn't make 'em! They wanted it!

CRYSTAL. Phil turned over a new leaf this morning. It scares me.

PHIL. I told 'em that. You know the first thing I did? I got my coat back.

RAY. I figured that was long gone.

PHIL. Look at it! I found the bum that was wearing it. He was sitting in a tree in the park. I saw my coat and I pulled the son of a bitch out of the tree and marched him out on the bridge. He was babbling like a baby. So I ripped my coat off him and threw him off the bridge. You want proof, you go look down off the bridge. You see the exact outline of a bum in the ice. He went right through it like a cookie-cutter. And I got my coat back.

CRYSTAL. It's not really your coat, honey.

PHIL. Okay, the lining's different. But the rest is just like my coat.

RAY. This bum didn't even take it?

PHIL. He would have if he had the chance. Son of a bitch.

CRYSTAL. Let's go, Phil. The Thimble Museum is only open 'til noon.

PHIL. (*To Ray and Faye.*) You'll get the stuff as soon as they send it to me. Just don't bug me about it 'cause I got a lot on my mind, okay?

(*PHIL and CRYSTAL exit. FAYE gets out the chowder and coffee. SHE and RAY start to eat.*)

FAYE. I been thinking, Ray. You burn Arnie's house and I steal all the tips, we could head outta here.

RAY. Where to?

FAYE. You know. Someplace warm. Someplace different. Wherever it is people go when they leave.

RAY. There's no place different than this, Faye. We get in the car, drive all night, stop someplace for breakfast and we're in the Hungry Pilgrim. Drive two more days, hole up someplace and we're living in this house. This is it. This is all there is. This is where I hear the voice.

FAYE. We're running out of time, Ray, can't you see that? We're sunk. No more rooms to close off, all the furniture burned and the house freezing up. You and me huddled here waiting for something to come down from the sky—

RAY. Goddammit, Faye! Here on top of this house my life got changed. I swear I'm gonna be here when it comes back.

FAYE. You're filled up with this hopeless longing and it's pulling us down, Ray—something's gotta be done.

ARNIE. (*Enters from outside. HE has a handful of soaking leaflets.*) What's with Phil? I'm coming up the walk, he steps outta the garage with a pistol, makes me kneel in the snow and buy shit out of the back of his car. You know somebody your whole life they shouldn't be using guns on you.

RAY. He's settling his accounts today. How'd you do, Arnie?

ARNIE. It's a battle out there. The whole damn mall was crawling with fanatics. I got roughed up by a bunch of drunken Hari Krishnas who took my space. Then I got squeezed between a herd of fundamentalists and some Moonies on a rampage. I finally get my own place and things are going okay until some guy douses himself with gasoline and lights himself on fire.

RAY. What the hell was that about?

ARNIE. Just a new shoe store opening up.

RAY. So you lost your crowd?

ARNIE. Everybody went to buy shoes. Then they were browsing from one cult to the next. We can match up with the others, Ray. We'll get us a helluva turn-out tonight, I bet.

FAYE. They're not coming here, I hope.

ARNIE. We had to put an address down on the flyer.

FAYE. Are you expecting me to feed them, Ray? Because I'm working all day—

RAY. Nah, we'll take care of everything. If there's too many, we'll head outside town to a big field. Build a bonfire.

BILL. (*Enters from making his calls.*) Is it any warmer in here?

FAYE. Maybe a little. What went?

BILL. Some chair.

RAY. (*Looking around the room.*) That was my favorite chair!

BILL. I don't know these things, Ray.

FAYE. It's not his fault, Ray. We should divide it all up—things we can burn and things we can sell.

BILL. That oughta cover everything.

RAY. I would have burned everything in the house before I burned that chair.

FAYE. Ray? Will you drive me to work? I don't wanna walk with the dogs out there.

RAY. We'll take Bill's car. You want to come with us, Arnie?

BILL. Don't bother goin' to work, Faye.

FAYE. How come?

BILL. The Hungry Pilgrim's closing early.

FAYE .Why?

BILL. Fire of suspicious origin. (*Glances at watch.*) In about one hour.

RAY. (*To Faye.*) Might as well skip it. How many tips you gonna get in an hour?

FAYE. That's not fair! I never got to be manager! They burn the place before I even get to work! It's got to stop, all this has got to stop. Ray, you do something. You stop it—

RAY. What can I do?

BILL. It's too late to stop. It's rolling along real good.

FAYE. What about me? What about what I want?

BILL. You're one person, Faye. What me and Ray are riding is public demand. They want this. They call in orders. When the demand stops, I'm gone to new territory. And Ray is out of work again. You oughta be glad the community is behind us.

FAYE. I never been in charge of anything. This here was my big break, my one chance to order people around and now it's all gone. (*FAYE rips off her Pilgrim outfit and jams it in the oven with the laundry that Ray put there earlier. Then SHE gets a glass of scotch. SHE sits in one of the few remaining chairs in her slip, drinking scotch.*)

RAY. I'm sorry, Faye. I'm just a guy trying to get by. That's all I am.

BILL. She'll get over it. You can't be thinking "Who works here?" "Who lives here?" every time you strike a match. You wouldn't be able to do your job.

ARNIE. I gotta work at the 7-Eleven this afternoon, Ray. We got any more cars to do?

RAY. There's a whole back-log. But you're flying solo.

ARNIE. Where you gonna be?

RAY. Bill got me another assignment. If I want to do it.

BILL. Ray's gonna burn your house down, Arnie.

ARNIE. What for?

BILL. Your landlord placed the order. You got time to get your things out if you haul ass.

ARNIE. You're really doing this to me, Ray? I mean that's where I live.

RAY. It's nothing personal, Arnie. It's just business. (*Beat.*) I'll even give you a taste of it. How's that?

BILL. That's a separate deal, Ray. That's your action, not mine.

RAY. What do you say, Arnie. Forty percent? (*To Bill.*) It's all for the church anyway.

BILL. You want trouble you won't have to look for.

ARNIE. What have I gotta do?

RAY. Nothing. It's just so there's no hard feelings.

ARNIE. What time?

BILL. Real soon. This afternoon. We gotta move quick.

ARNIE. That could be a problem. My wife's got a doctor's appointment.

BILL. A deal is a deal.

RAY. You got time to tell your wife and get your things out. Forty percent, for Chrissakes.

ARNIE. What the hell. She wanted to move anyway. I'll see you tonight, Ray. (*Exits.*)

(FAYE sits apart from Bill and Ray, drinking her scotch. BILL gets a necktie from his pocket and puts it on.)

BILL. I'm goin' to a meeting over at the Holiday Inn. We're closing in on something big. First time they ever let me sit at the table.

RAY. Where do you usually sit?

BILL. I'm the guy that gets to the meeting early. Plant listening devices, maybe stick some plastic explosives in a briefcase, knock somebody off when they're getting out of their car, that kind of thing. This time they're gonna prop me up at the conference table like a person. It makes me feel damn good, I'll tell you.

RAY. What have you got going? Another block?

BILL Let's just say this one is so big it involves foreigners, you know, people with accents. Ray, make me proud of you this afternoon and I'll get you on board.

RAY. I never done a house.

BILL. It's the best. A three-decker's like a week in bed with a beautiful woman. Use the skills you already got. Drive a car into the basement and let it go. Knock on apartment 1-B. Get a receipt and the money's yours.

RAY. That don't sound so bad.

BILL. But get right on it. Some free agent gets there first, you miss out on a big pay-day.

RAY. You got the contract.

BILL. Open your eyes, Ray. There are people out there who ain't playin' by the rules, got no respect for a contract. It makes it tough for the rest of us. Don't let me know anything else about that church of yours. I tell you this for your own good.

(BILL puts on his overcoat and exits. FAYE starts trying to clean the room.)

RAY. Don't touch that stuff!

FAYE. I can't live with it anymore!

RAY. We need it for tonight.

FAYE. I get burned out of my job. I lose my house to some kind of spirits in the night. I don't know why I should stay here anymore, Ray. I really don't.

RAY. We're on the verge of something, Faye. Just give it a chance.

FAYE. I need a job. But I don't know where to go because I don't know what's going to get burned next. I don't wanna get a job and then find out that you're torching the joint. It's stupid to get a full-time job unless it's gonna last a couple of days.

RAY. Maybe you could sign on with Bill. He's the only one that knows what's gonna be left in town.

FAYE. You want me to work for Bill?

RAY. There's a lot to be done. Filing, keeping the books, all that stuff. Their office is in bad shape. It hurts business. People call to place an order and they spend half the day on hold. I could talk to him.

FAYE. That's okay. I'll talk to him.

RAY. Just talk, right? I mean, you just talk to him.

FAYE. That's right. I'll talk to him.

RAY. You and Bill. What's the story, Faye?

FAYE. He's your boss. He's okay. I mean he's got you back working again, right?

RAY. You gotta promise me something, Faye. When I ask you about Bill ... when I got some booze in me and I'm demanding some answers ... when you see my hand in a fist and veins sticking out on my neck and I'm screaming for the truth, you lie to me, okay?

FAYE. Okay.

RAY. Promise?

FAYE. Yeah, I promise I'll lie.

RAY. Thanks. (*Puts on his coat.*) Do I look okay?

FAYE. You look like you always do. Why?

RAY. It's my first house, Faye. Wish me luck.

(RAY exits. FAYE goes back to her scotch. We hear the rising sound of DOGS barking outside as the LIGHTS fade to black.)

Scene 2

(FAYE is making more coffee. SHE's wearing a coat over her slip. BILL is back from his meeting. HE's sitting on the floor. FAYE brings him a cup of coffee and sits in one of the few remaining chairs.)

BILL. I never been treated so good as I was at this meeting. I go into the conference room and there at everybody's place is a legal pad, a sharpened pencil, and a mint. Can you beat that? A fucking mint. I'd say my days undercover are over.

FAYE. Undercover? You mean you're a cop?

BILL. Don't make me laugh. I don't even talk to cops anymore. Cops get their orders from people a helluva lot lower than me in the company. *(HE drinks the coffee.)* I talk to people that matter. Like foreigners. They're gonna give me the big job. Ray does it and we ride outta here on his back, you know what I'm saying?

FAYE. They're transferring you?

BILL. Depends how I do the job. They're either gonna give me a promotion or rub me out. I got a feeling in my gut it's a promotion. I wanna share it with you, Faye. Take you to Florida with me.

FAYE. You want to just leave?

BILL. The territory's used up. The smart money heads for new turf.

FAYE .What about Ray?

BILL. I'm your ticket outta here, you know that. (*Beat.*) Best thing I ever did was read that ad you put in the paper. I was hitting up everybody with a car to sell, just to get the business moving. I never thought I'd find my whole work-force and the love of my life on the other end of that ad. (*Beat.*) Think about it, Faye. Florida. With the right breaks, I could make things very normal for you.

FAYE. It's warm down there. I'd like that.

BILL. I'll have me a rock-solid desk job and a house that looks like every other house. Mow the lawn on weekends. Sundays sit in a normal church and worship a normal god. I won't even have to go out in the field. Just set things up clean, hire the right people, and keep everybody happy. I'll pay my people well, give them a share of the pot. I worked my whole life in this company and I never got no breaks. Now that I've made it, I'm ready to share the wealth in return for loyalty. Loyalty, trust, that's the foundation of a good business. The more you can trust your people, the more you can have a life of your own. I've worked hard my whole life, Faye. Now it's time to enjoy things.

RAY. (*Enters from outside. HE locks the door and hands Bill the receipt.*) Did you hear it? Lord, it was something. I found a Chevy that was double-parked, blasted it right through into the basement and set it going. I got the receipt and watched the fire tearing through the building. The flames hit the gas main and just shot up into the sky like a rocket to outer space. Then this explosion shook the whole block and windows dropped out up and down the street and a wave of heat pushed me away. I wish you'd have been there, Faye, it's the best thing I ever done.

FAYE. Did anyone see you?

RAY. See me? Oh, yeah. The crowd kept getting bigger and bigger, just standing there in the rain watching and you could see it in their eyes they were followers. Faye, if I can get 'em all together with just a two-bit housefire, think what I can do when they see I got the voice of truth in my head. You're helping me get to the other side, Bill. You don't even know it, but that's what you're doing.

FAYE. Arnie make it out okay?

RAY. I was calling out to him, but I don't know. There were sirens blaring and people screaming. He had time if he moved quick. (*To Bill.*) I done you proud, Bill. You owe me the big one.

BILL. Don't you worry. I'm gonna take real good care of you, Ray.

(*BILL opens his briefcase and gets out a voucher, letting Ray again see the stacks of money. HE hands the voucher to Ray. There's a POUNDING at the door.*)

BILL. Somebody follow you or what?

RAY. Nobody followed me.

BILL. (*Goes to the door. Calling out.*) Get the hell away from here!

PHIL. (*From outside.*) Let us in! Hurry!

(*BILL opens the door. PHIL and CRYSTAL burst in. PHIL is wearing a dress. THEY are carrying armfuls of loaves of bread, which THEY throw on the floor. BILL locks the door again.*)

BILL. What are you doing?

PHIL. A cop was shooting at us.

CRYSTAL. Police brutality.

BILL. What for?

PHIL. Beats me. Scared the hell out of us. They shouldn't have guns the way they use 'em on innocent people.

RAY. This was the field trip?

CRYSTAL. We didn't go. There was a run on the orphans today. Some women's group showed up to take 'em to the ballet. There was a lot of pushing and shoving, and we finally grabbed enough orphans to take to the Thimble Museum. Then we found out that Lowell is burning.

BILL. What did you say?

PHIL. There's fires raging right through downtown. The traffic is a bitch.

BILL. Those bastards. I own Lowell! They gave me the option at the meeting! I paid good money for it!

RAY. Lowell was the big job, right? It was s'posed to be mine.

BILL. Maybe I'm getting set up ... they call me into the meeting and sell me Lowell when it's already half-burned. What kind of bullshit is that?

RAY. Who's doing it?

BILL. Who the hell knows? A bunch of people having a bad day. I heard rumors but I didn't think it would come to this.

RAY. Well if you bought the option—

BILL. I got it right here!

RAY. Maybe we oughta do something.

FAYE. Like what?

RAY. Like move on these people. Clear 'em out so we can burn it right.

BILL. I'm not gonna stoop to their level, Ray. It just makes me mad. You get people who are not trained professionals burning up a town it could cause real problems.

RAY. So what are you gonna do?

BILL. Pick up the pace here in town. These crazy bastards beat us to it then the whole territory is worthless. So we have to take it out first at reduced rates. Cut our profit margin so we can stay in the game. (*To Phil.*) Downtown Lowell is gone? There's nothing worth torching?

PHIL. That's what we heard.

BILL. I had it in my pocket. I was gonna be the guy that took Lowell off the map. Maybe I'll take a drive over, scope it out.

CRYSTAL. I wouldn't do that.

BILL. Why not?

CRYSTAL. Everything's on fire. You'll never get close.

BILL. I shoulda known from last night. I drove over to check things out. I'm feeling mighty proud, seeing all them buildings ready to come down just 'cause of me. But I smelled something wrong. There's all these people out on the streets, walking real fast. I stop at a light and I see 'em surround somebody and go to work. It wasn't just kids doing the stomping, hell, that's a normal part of growing up. It was guys in suits, check-out girls from the supermarket, bank-tellers, guys that sell shoes. The whole goddam town was out there in the middle of the night breaking windows and beating the shit out of each other but they sure weren't torching anything.

PHIL. They are now. Lowell is history.

RAY. What I'm hearing is that I'm not gonna get my big chance.

BILL. Don't give up so quick, Ray. In my line of work there's always a solution. (*BILL starts checking his papers.*)

FAYE. I like the dress, Phil.

CRYSTAL. We went creepy-crawling in Phil's house and stole all his wife's clothes.

PHIL. That oughta show her! She won't buy my products then I'm gonna steal her clothes. Fair is fair.

CRYSTAL. Then we were driving around when we decided to drop by the 7-Eleven to see Arnie.

PHIL. But he wasn't there, so we decided we might as well hold up the place. I mean we got a gun, right? We go out to the car and I put on this dress so no one will know me. We go back in and there's a long line of people waiting to pay. Soon as they see the gun they just start grabbing things off the shelves and running out to their cars without paying—

CRYSTAL. Smart shoppers.

PHIL. We take the bread and some cop starts blasting away at us like we're common criminals and we came over here.

FAYE. I thought you were gonna win the trip to France.

PHIL. I'm through selling. Amway's dead in the water.

CRYSTAL. Phil decided he isn't a people person.

PHIL. The mood in our community has really turned ugly. I figured I flash the piece and my sales curve heads north. No way. These people see the gun and they're all set to fight back. Men, women, kids, everybody wants to be a fucking hero.

BILL. You gonna run around in a dress holding up stores?

PHIL. There aren't too many left open. Crystal thought I could get work with you.

BILL. That what she thought?

PHIL. She said you already talked it over.

BILL. Oh, yeah. We had a nice long talk. We explored each others feelings on the subject. It was a good meeting. Lots of give and take. She gave and I took. Right, Crystal?

(PHIL looks from Bill to Crystal. FAYE gets up and takes the bread to the kitchen. SHE starts buttering the bread.)

PHIL. What'd you decide?

BILL. I'll interview you, Phil. But I make no promises. Sit down.

(PHIL sits on the trunk. BILL sits across from him like a formal job interview.)

BILL. So ... how are we doing today?

PHIL. Fine. Thanks.

BILL. Now ... tell me a little bit about yourself.

PHIL. C'mon, Bill. You know who I am.

BILL. Don't tell a man how to run his business. Why should I hire you?

PHIL. Well ... I know I could handle the work. I've been a lawyer and a salesman and I worked in the plant a long time. I'm separated and currently living in my car. I lived in town my whole life so I know the area real good. The main thing is, I need this job so bad I'll do whatever you ask, no questions. Plus, I carry a gun.

BILL. You ever burn anything before?

PHIL. Not professionally. Just some hell-raising out at the quarry. Years ago. 'Member, Ray?

RAY. Yeah, but they never caught us.

BILL. Where do you hope to be in five years?

PHIL. For starters, I'd like to be living indoors. Anything after that is gravy.

BILL. I want you to fill out this application and return it at your earliest convenience.

PHIL. Thanks. (*PHIL is completing the application when there's a KNOCKING at the door.*)

BILL. Who the hell is that?

FAYE. Maybe it's your followers, Ray. They got this address.

PHIL. You want me to shoot 'em, Bill?

BILL. Maybe. We'll see. (*Going to the door.*) Who is it?

ARNIE. C'mon, open up! (*ARNIE enters. HE's soaking wet and shivering.*)

RAY. Hey, Arnie.

ARNIE. Thanks for giving me time to get outta my house, Ray.

RAY. What do you mean? You had time.

ARNIE. I was in there when you done it!

PHIL. Done what?

ARNIE. Ray burned down my house.

CRYSTAL. That's nice.

RAY. Arnie, I can't believe you didn't have time to get out. Bill, give him forty percent, would you?

(BILL writes out a voucher for Arnie.)

ARNIE. I'm standing there trying to explain to my wife about the contract, how we get forty percent of Ray's fee, right? But she couldn't understand. I guess she was feeling down in the mouth at her doctor's appointment so he gives her some pills to boost her spirits. Then we hear the big bang in the basement. I tried to throw her out the window but she wouldn't budge. I figured even if I did get her out the window she wouldn't have sense to drop to the ground she was so spaced. So we took the stairs. The crowd—

PHIL. She okay now, Arnie?

ARNIE. She took the whole thing pretty good, considering. Right now she's just wandering around downtown kind of looking at things. I'm s'posed to meet her tonight. We'll have a drink and figure where to live.

CRYSTAL. We've got room in the car.

BILL. Where you meeting her?

ARNIE. Holiday Inn.

BILL. What time?

ARNIE. Ten o'clock.

BILL. Better make it earlier. There won't be no Holiday Inn at ten o'clock.

ARNIE. I'll track her down and tell her. She's flexible.

BILL. Sit tight, I'll be back. If things fall right then you're on board, Phil.

(BILL exits. FAYE enters with several trays of buttered bread.)

RAY. Thanks, hon. You didn't have to do this.

FAYE. I know. It's just been so long since we had people over for dinner.

(THEY all start eating the bread.)

FAYE. Arnie, you're making me cold just standing there soaked.

RAY. I got some clothes in the oven you can wear, Arnie.

ARNIE. Thanks. (*Goes to the kitchen. HE pulls Faye's Pilgrim outfit out of the oven.*) The Pilgrim really went under, Faye?

FAYE. Oh, yeah. I'm through with that place for good.

(ARNIE strips down and puts on Ray's clothes from the oven. They are charred and smoking.)

ARNIE. I quit too. Fired is maybe a better word. Your clothes are done, Ray.

PHIL. We stopped by to see you, Arnie.

CRYSTAL. You weren't there.

ARNIE. I went in early to buy some bread. I'm standing in line, I mean people must be stocking up on supplies or something—

PHIL. That's about the only store still open.

ARNIE. Anyway, I get to the front of the line, pay for the bread, and the new manager gives me the change and fires me. Just like that. I heard they were going for new blood at the 7-Eleven, but that's a cold way to do business. Didn't even call me at home.

PHIL. You shoulda waited. Me and Crystal got the line moving. Didn't we, baby-doll?

(PHIL and CRYSTAL kiss. RAY opens the trunk.

FAYE. It never used to be like this. Nothing ever was like it is now.

RAY. This was the kind of day when I first heard it. Heavy rain and that feeling in your gut that the whole world is splitting apart.

ARNIE. You gonna try to hear it, Ray?

RAY. Find what's left of the pizza, would you?

PHIL. Don't you think you better save it for tonight, Ray? I mean if there's really people coming over—

RAY. It won't wait, Phil. All I can do is listen.

(PHIL and ARNIE look for the pizza on the floor. RAY puts on the helmet. FAYE goes to the kitchen.)

CRYSTAL. Faye? Do you need any help?

FAYE. Thanks, that's nice of you to offer.

(CRYSTAL and FAYE start buttering more bread. RAY turns on the helmet and the lights start BLINKING. ARNIE dims the lights. THEY strip off their shirts. ARNIE and PHIL kneel in front of Ray. RAY takes a bite of the pizza and hands it to PHIL and ARNIE, who also take a bite.)

RAY. The True Value Church is now in session.

(Pause.)

ARNIE. You hearing anything, Ray?

RAY. (*Pause.*) I am! I'm hearing it! Things are happening ... turning around ... we're getting back to what it was before. I see Arnie, he's driving, picking up me and Phil. It's the morning, seven-thirty, dew on the grass, Phil's got three King Buds. We crack 'em and start drinking ... then we're at the factory. It's opened up and we got our jobs back. We're there in the plant, doing the straight eight, the clock is crawling and we're aching for the week-end. It's what life is and it's coming back. I smell that factory smell and I see all them faces, the eyes just staring ... we're going back, all of us. The sound, all them machines beating out some kind of rhythm that gets stuck in your head, so you wake up in the night and you hear it, clear as if you were still at the plant. (*Beat.*) This is no dream I'm having. This is real. Phil, Arnie, we're going back to work. You know what this means? The long nightmare is over! The new day is starting for us!

(RAY takes off the helmet. ARNIE turns on the light.)

RAY. Faye! The plant's opening up!
FAYE. (*Calling from the kitchen.*) How do you know?
RAY. I heard it and it's true.
ARNIE. What was it like, Ray?
RAY. It was the truth, Arnie, like a warm hand around my heart. I got no doubts. Shit, we oughta celebrate! Bring some beers!

(FAYE and CRYSTAL enter with bread and beer.)

FAYE. Don't be saying this if it isn't true, Ray. We've waited so goddam long.

RAY. You remember how it used to be? Life just pulled us along, every week like the last one.

FAYE. It was steady. It was normal. Pay off the bills the day they come—

ARNIE. Oh, yeah, a regular pay-check, buy whatever you want, take years to pay it off—

CRYSTAL. I wish I'd been around then.

RAY. Don't worry, it's gonna be the same except better.

FAYE. I remember how warm it used to be in here. We'd have all the rooms open and before the chimney went bad we had fires in the fireplace, where they oughta be.

BILL. (*Enters from outside.*) Everybody listen up real good. The whole town's going. The mayor signed the papers, the insurance is all in order, now the real work begins.

RAY. With all due respect, Bill, I have to ask you to get the fuck out of my house.

ARNIE. We're through with your operation.

BILL. You want me to leave? *(HE stares at them.)* For Chrissakes, don't you know what's happening? Those bastards from Lowell are coming across the bridge, a whole long line of 'em, torching everything in sight. They get to town first, then the whole thing's gonna go for nothing, just out of the sickness in their hearts. These aren't pros, this is amateur night, it's nothing but a goddam riot.

FAYE. The town's been sold?

BILL. We burn it for money or they burn it for kicks.

RAY. It got sold cheap, I bet.

BILL. We still turn a profit.

RAY. What about the factory? It's opening up, isn't it?

BILL. How'd you hear? Nobody's s'posed to know that.

RAY. Look at me, Bill. I got TV in my head. I got voices from the future, I got a direct line upstairs. You hear this, Faye? You thought it wasn't real, but it's happening, just like I said. The factory's opening up again.

BILL. That's why they want it burned. These are the people I told you about, Ray. Foreigners. They're ready to give you the job of a lifetime.

ARNIE. Why should we do that? Then we can't work there.

BILL. You know what it's like when a plastics factory goes? It's only about the most beautiful thing you could see in your life. It lights up the sky with a million colors. You can just lie on your back staring up in the sky and it's like going drinking with God.

RAY. Get outta here, Bill. We want our old life back and we're gonna get it.

BILL. I'll be straight with you. I made a commitment to take care of the factory. The company is counting on me.

FAYE. What happens if you don't do it?

BILL. I get a bullet in the head. Now I can live with that, I'm not a goddam baby. That's the downside, getting your head blown to pieces because the work isn't done on time. But you gotta look at the upside of this operation. For me, I pull this sucker out of the hat with all the shit that's coming down and they will give me Florida, the whole fucking state, no restrictions. I will burn it surgically, a theme park here, a marina there, and that is my life's work. Florida will take me into my old age.

RAY. You get Florida and we barely get a living wage for burning our factory.

BILL. You wanna know what I'll give you? I'll give you Lowell.

PHIL. Lowell?

RAY. Who wants Lowell? It's all burned up.

BILL. Ray, you don't know the business, so you give up. I've set up Lowell so it's like a fucking annuity for you and your Church.

ARNIE. What's this got to do with the Church?

BILL. I got a contractor going into Lowell as soon as the rubble cools down. He's putting up six square miles of condos, identical units. The people who had their houses burned are putting their insurance checks right into the condos, so he's got ninety percent occupancy in three months. But the kicker is, I extended the option, so we're talking about six square miles of condos that are pre-built, pre-burned, and you're holding the papers. Plus, since my life is on the line, I'll throw in exclusive renewal rights. You can burn it over and over the rest of your lives.

RAY. I'm not burning the plant. That was our life and it's gonna be our life all over again.

FAYE. He's telling you it's over, it's going to get burned anyway—

RAY. It ain't over, Faye! You remember how good our life used to be?

FAYE. Don't be talking like that, Ray. You had this hope growing inside me and now it's gone again.

BILL. Twenty years of double-shifts you won't make the money I'm giving you right now.

PHIL. Jesus, Ray.

CRYSTAL. We could get a little place of our own, Phil. Out by the lake.

ARNIE. And the Church, that oughta be for everybody. This could be the best thing that ever happened to us—

(RAY and BILL are facing each other, only feet apart.)

RAY. I already saw the best thing that ever happened to us. We were working together, bringing home a regular pay-check, building some kind of a life. It all got taken away. By guys like you.

BILL. I'm *giving* you something, Ray. I'm giving you all you need for a decent life. The whole world forgot about you guys and here you are, turning down the last chance you got left. (*Beat.*) You move on this deal now or it's gone forever.

RAY. We're through gettin' our hands dirty for you.

BILL. My hands are clean. (*BILL slowly holds up his hands, open, in front of him, palms facing Ray.*) How about you, Ray? Are your hands clean?

(RAY puts up his hands, palms facing Bill. BILL takes Ray's hands and starts bending them back as RAY struggles. For a moment the outcome is in doubt, then BILL forces RAY back onto the one remaining chair. BILL releases his hands. RAY and BILL are still staring at each other.)

RAY. They got you, Bill.

BILL. Yeah? Who's got me?

RAY. *(In his own world.)* I see 'em in the streets, their faces twisted in a rage they don't understand. Their eyes pressed up against the glass, burning right into you. Hands reaching for you, pulling you out onto the street. And it sure don't end there. You waited too long, Bill. You shoulda left.

BILL. We lost him, boys. Poor crazy bastard. The world just ain't enough for some people. (*Beat.*) Phil, I want you and Arnie riding in the back of my pick-up—

CRYSTAL. Can I come too? I want to see the sky afterwards.

BILL. Sure, you can help 'em out. Soon as the plant is burning, haul ass out, get in the truck, and I'll drive you anywhere you wanna go.

ARNIE. We'll see you later on, Ray. At the meeting.

(PHIL, CRYSTAL and ARNIE exit.)

BILL. Faye, I'll need you along to take care of the paperwork. (*To Ray.*) You know what a religious leader is that's got no followers? A lunatic, that's what. Your average nut house is full of them, just like you. (*Beat.*) Hang in there, Ray. We'll be back before you know it. (*BILL takes the helmet, unseen by Ray, and exits.*)

FAYE. Will you come with us, Ray?

RAY. I saw it all so clear, what we used to have. It don't have to end.

(FAYE crosses to the door.)

RAY. You're really going with him?

FAYE. I'm working for him just like you wanted.

RAY. It's just work, right? Like I been doing?

FAYE. That's right, Ray. It's just work.

RAY. The factory is open. You can't doubt me anymore. I'm chosen, just like I said.

*(FAYE exits, and RAY is left alone in the room.
BLACKOUT. We hear the rising sound of the DOGS
outside, occasional SIRENS, and a distant MOB.)*

Scene 3

*(The SOUNDS from outside fade as the LIGHTS come up.
ARNIE, PHIL, and CRYSTAL enter from outside. Their
clothes are grimy and they are all exhausted. RAY stares
at them.)*

ARNIE. Well, we done it.

PHIL. You shoulda been there, Ray. I never saw so
many people.

CRYSTAL. And none of 'em have houses anymore. Or
cars. It makes me realize how lucky we are, Phil.

ARNIE. It wasn't just for us, Ray. It was for the
Church.

PHIL. The people cheered us like heroes when we came
out —

ARNIE. Things were exploding all around, each one
bigger than the last, 'til the whole thing blows up—

CRYSTAL. The sky was just like he said—

ARNIE. And everybody was staring up at it with this
look of wonder, like it was pulling 'em right up outta
themselves.

RAY. Where's Faye?

ARNIE. They weren't there when we came out.

CRYSTAL. They were the getaway car. They were supposed to wait.

PHIL. We were kind of hoping they'd have come back here.

CRYSTAL. We ran all the way back—

(RAY exits to the bedroom. CRYSTAL goes to the window and stares out.)

PHIL. I can't believe he stiffed us for the money and left us cold. What are we s'posed to do?

ARNIE. Wish we'd have seen my wife out there.

PHIL. She's okay, Arnie. I bet she went to the Holiday Inn, saw it wasn't there, and figured you'd changed your plans.

CRYSTAL. Phil, we gotta get out of here. The money was the only reason to stay. The people out there scare me.

PHIL. Maybe Bill's coming back. Then we get our money—

CRYSTAL. He's gone, Phil. We got to get away—

PHIL. I don't want to just leave—

CRYSTAL. They taught me stuff in rehab, Phil, about taking care of my life, not getting pushed around. I have real worth as a human being. I plan to learn a trade that takes advantage of today's technology. I can do anything, I can learn to install telephones in cars. I'm going, Phil. I want you to come with me.

PHIL. Where would we go?

CRYSTAL. Don't try to confuse me, Phil. I know I'm right. They told us to be self-reliant. I was a quick learner.

PHIL. Come here, Crystal.

CRYSTAL. Are you coming with me?

PHIL. Let's talk about it.

CRYSTAL. (*SHE pulls out the gun.*) There's no time to talk.

PHIL. Would you put that away! I only gave it to you 'cause you were the look-out.

CRYSTAL. The car keys, Phil.

PHIL. You want the keys to my car? That's my domicile, honey. That holds all my worldly possessions.

(CRYSTAL fires a warning shot over Phil's head. PHIL and ARNIE hit the floor.)

ARNIE. Would you give her the goddam keys? She doesn't want to talk.

(PHIL tosses Crystal the keys.)

CRYSTAL. Come here, Phil.

PHIL. Don't shoot me, Crystal. You can have the car.

CRYSTAL. Closer, Phil.

(PHIL moves closer to Crystal.)

CRYSTAL. Gimme a hug.

(THEY embrace, CRYSTAL holding the gun to his ribs as THEY kiss.)

CRYSTAL. Tell me you understand.

PHIL. It's okay, Crystal. I understand.

CRYSTAL. I knew you would. You been real good to me. (*SHE pulls away.*) Back on the floor, Phil.

PHIL. Crystal? Does this mean we're through?

(CRYSTAL fires another warning shot, then exits to the garage.)

PHIL. No woman treats me like that. She better not even think of coming back.

(RAY enters from the hall.)

ARNIE. Ray? You think we oughta make a run for it?

PHIL. I'd offer my car but Crystal took it.

RAY. She left too?

PHIL. That's what the gunshots were. We broke up.

RAY. You guys can leave if you want.

ARNIE. I'm with you, Ray. The Church is everything.

PHIL. And we still got Lowell, just as soon as they build it.

ARNIE. You okay?

RAY. I never thought she'd leave me. I tried to tell her to wait. Things were gonna get better.

ARNIE. She didn't understand. If she understood, she never would have left.

PHIL. Could you maybe try to hear it again, Ray?

ARNIE. I need it real bad. (*Beat.*) We shoulda listened to you, Ray. We never should have gone with him.

PHIL. It's in the air, I mean if you heard it earlier I bet you can hear it again—

RAY. It's gone. The helmet's gone.

ARNIE. What do you mean?

RAY. I left it right here and now it's gone.

PHIL. Let's try to catch him! Get it back!

ARNIE. It's over. All that's left is real life.

(CRYSTAL enters from outside.)

PHIL. Crystal! What's going on?

CRYSTAL. The car wouldn't start. *(Beat.)* I think we should get married.

PHIL. You want to marry me?

CRYSTAL. I'm sorry I was shooting at you, Phil. I've just felt edgy all day.

PHIL. I'm just glad to have you back. My life has been absolute hell without you.

(PHIL and CRYSTAL start to make out on the floor. FAYE enters from outside. SHE has two six-packs of beer, a pizza, clothes, and food. From outside, we hear the sound of a distant MOB, occasionally punctuated by SIRENS.)

FAYE. You boys dry?

RAY. Thought you were gone, Faye. Thought you left me cold.

FAYE. Soon as they went into the factory he drove off like a wild-man. We were going to Florida. I made him drop me at the light on Main, said I forgot something.

RAY. He still waiting?

FAYE. I don't know, I ran like hell. They surrounded his car and started rocking it back and forth. Everyone I ever saw in my life is out on the streets tonight. I saw your wife, Arnie.

ARNIE. Where is she? Is she okay?

FAYE. She's fine. The rain is finally turning to snow ... everybody's all bundled up. But there she was, walking alone in a nice summer dress, no coat, smiling and happy. I went over to her and she wasn't even wet from the rain. She looked so pretty.

ARNIE. What's she doing?

FAYE. Shopping, just like everybody else.

PHIL. I thought the stores were all closed.

FAYE. Now they're all open, permanently. (*SHE puts the groceries on the counter*.) The best thing is, you don't even need money. You just go in and take what you want. Look at the stuff I got.

RAY. I'm glad you came back, Faye.

FAYE. The thought of you opening the refrigerator and finding no beer, it about broke my heart.

(THEY open the beers and start drinking.)

FAYE. You've got your work cut out, Ray. The people are heading this way.

RAY. What people is that?

(The SOUNDS from outside are growing louder.)

FAYE. Your people. Some of 'em had flyers from the mall. They got this address and they're on their way. That's why I got the pizza. I figured you need it for the ceremony.

RAY. There's no ceremony. I can't do it.

ARNIE. You gotta do something, Ray. They want it bad.

FAYE. I opened the car door and just got swept along by the mob coming this way. The way they talk they already believe.

RAY. What am I gonna do? I got nothing.

PHIL. You think we oughta try to leave?

RAY. We can't out-run this, it's everywhere.

ARNIE. You had nothing the first time, Ray.

FAYE. The fires will be burning for days. Nobody lives anywhere anymore. They need whatever you can give 'em.

RAY. Who the hell am I to talk to 'em?

FAYE. That voice wasn't coming from out there, Ray. It was coming from you, the whole time. That's why I came back. I saw those people out there and I knew you had the truth.

(The door opens and BILL enters, bloody and staggering. Through the open door we hear the sound of the MOB much louder. BILL stumbles and falls to the floor.)

BILL. I saw it ... just like you said ... the rage in the faces and the eyes burning through me and the hands all over me ... if it don't end there then where does it end? You gotta tell us where it ends, Ray ... you gotta tell us ... we got nowhere left to go ...

(BILL lies still. RAY is apart from the group, pressing his hands against his head as if to block out a deafening sound that only he can hear. The MOB outside is now very close. There are SIRENS and occasional GUNSHOTS. We hear an EXPLOSION and the LIGHTS in the house go out. Outside the window we see the flickering lights of the FIRES in town.)

RAY. I'm hearing it ... stronger than ever. But now it's more than one voice ... I'm hearing all kinds of voices, tangled up with each other, coming from all kinds of places. Screams rising up out of cold basements, angry voices in the night, whispers drifting in from the farms outta town, loud voices ripping outta the projects, dead voices, fighting their way out of all them boarded up houses, voices trying to explain themselves, how they feel and how they hurt and love and now they're all coming together in one de-ranged choir ... filling my head with one big voice ...

(The VOICES outside are rising. RAY rips off his shirt and goes to the window.)

RAY. I gotta talk to 'em ... tell 'em it's okay ... it's all gonna be okay. We got better days ahead. I gotta give 'em the word.

(As RAY opens the window, the SOUNDS from outside reach a peak ... the voices of the mob, the sirens, and the insane howling of the dogs. RAY climbs outside, and we see him scramble up on the roof, bare-chested in the night. It's snowing. RAY stares up into the sky in a moment of perfect peace as the SOUNDS fade to silence.)

BLACKOUT

THE END

COSTUME PLOT

<u>RAY</u>
ACT I
khaki work pants, beige belt, grey thick socks, work
    boots, green thermal shirt, green plaid flannel shirt, red
    plaid shirt jacket, watch
ACT II
brown overalls, black watchcap, goggles, black wool scarf,
    navy sweatshirt, work gloves, brown nylon jacket

<u>ARNIE</u>
ACT I
blue jeans, black belt, grey thick socks, red/white/navy
    polo shirt, black sneakers, navy quilted vest, purple
    "Lexington" jacket, full face mask, watch cap
ACT II
red nylon jacket, olive bandana, "charred" blue plaid shirt,
    athletic tee shirts

<u>FAYE</u>
ACT I
Pilgrim dress w/ belt, black Pilgrim shoes, purple down
    coat, purple gloves, purple/white scarf, plastic rainhat.,
    wedding band, pantyhose, black purse, pink/black dress,
    black high-heel pumps, pink/silver earrings
ACT II
black slip, dark pink bathrobe, patterned slipper socks, blue
    cardigan sweater, black mini skirt, black/green sweater

PHIL
ACT I

crumpled brown suit, blue plaid shirt, brown dotted tie, black belt, brown socks, brown loafers, rubber galoshes

ACT II

add brown overcoat w/ blue plaid lining, magenta 2-piece dress, wool tweed cap, blue bandana, green plaid shirt, paper respirator

CRYSTAL
ACT I

distressed jeans, distressed tee shirt, pale blue flannel plaid shirt, beige socks, distressed brown jacket, distressed sneakers

ACT II

add white panties, good jeans, cowboy boots, Phil's Act I blue plaid shirt, pea coat, earrings, black sweater, green print blouse, red bandana, paper respirator

BILL
ACT I

2-piece grey suit, white/blue striped shirt, grey/blue tie, gold watch, black Pierre Cardin belt, black tie shoes, grey dress socks, white handkerchief, grey/taupe wool scarf, black leather gloves, taupe winter trench coat

ACT II

remove good trench coat, add distressed trench coat

PROPERTY PLOT

<u>ACT I</u>
table
3 wooden chairs
TV
2 arm chairs
1 kitchen stool
oven mitt
3 towels
basket of wet laundry
beer cans
Boston newspaper
beers
bottle of whiskey
4 glasses
bottle of aspirin
box of baking soda
box with 3 dog sticks
2 gal. water jugs
4 coffee mugs
spoons/knives
napkins
bag of fast food
sample case w/Amway samples (carpet cleaner can, air
    freshener can, scissors/shoe polish (PHIL)
briefcase w/4 slices of pizza (PHIL)
briefcase w/money, vouchers, notebook, brush, aftershave
    (BILL)
penny (ARNIE)
pack of smack (BILL)
money (BILL)
keys/matches (BILL)
pizza slice (BILL)
football helmet w/antennae & Christmas lights

bag of dead animals

ACT II

newspaper (BILL)
flower (BILL)
toothbrush (CRYSTAL)
baking soda (CRYSTAL)
gas can (RAY)
voucher (BILL)
notebook (BILL)
chowder (in take-out bag) (FAYE)
leaflets (ARNIE)
bottle of scotch (FAYE)
coffee maker (BILL)
coffee mug (FAYE)
receipt (RAY)
loaves of bread (CRYSTAL)
gun, loaded/blanks (PHIL)
butter/knives (FAYE, CRYSTAL)
application form (BILL/PHIL)
charred clothes (ARNIE)
gun (CRYSTAL)
keys (PHIL)
2 six-packs (FAYE)
clothing from shopping (FAYE)
pizza (FAYE)
garbage can (under sink)
frozen shirt (bedroom)
squirt bottle

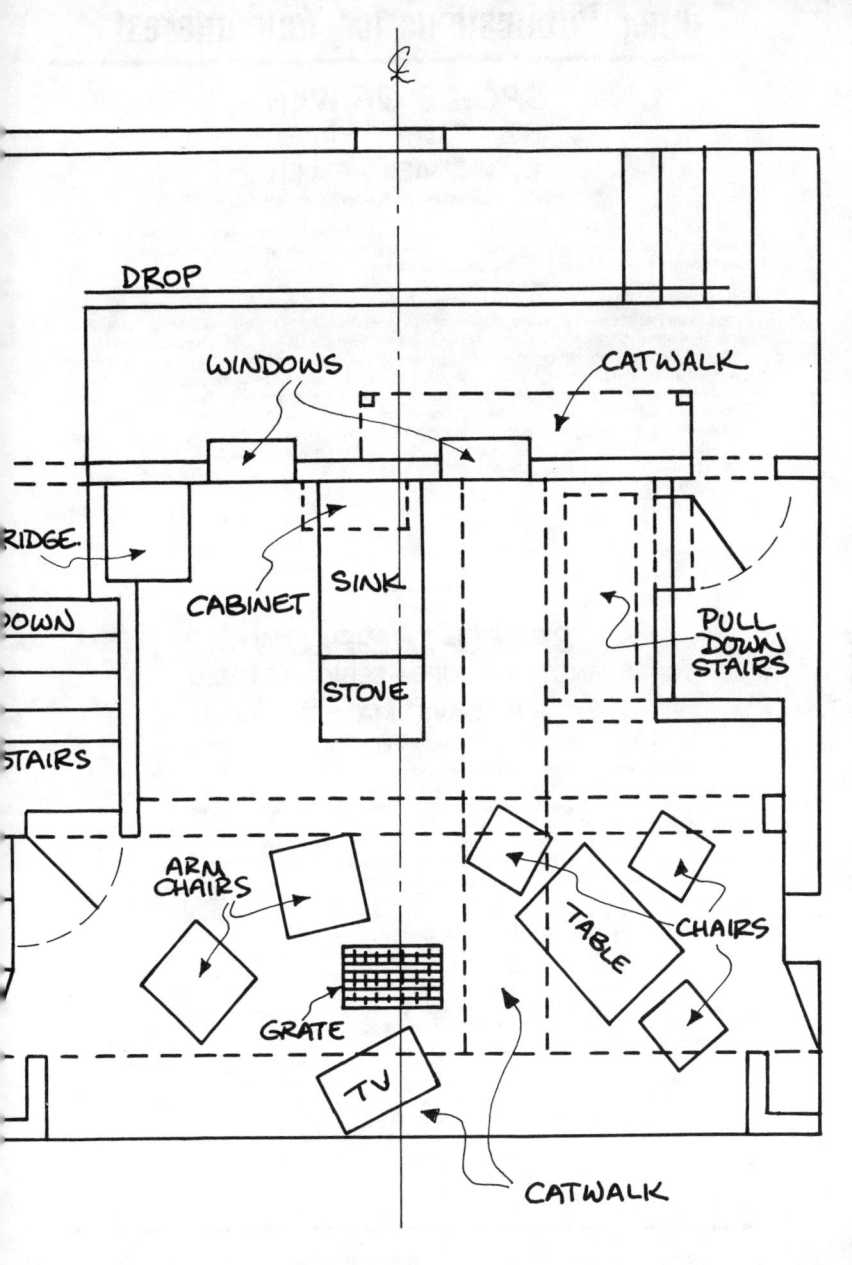

Other Publications for Your Interest

SPOILS OF WAR
(LITTLE THEATRE—DRAMA)

By MICHAEL WELLER
3 men, 3 women—Various Interior settings

Heretofore best known as the author of trenchant, bittersweet comedies such as *Loose Ends* and *Moonchildren*, as well as the screenplays for *Hair* and *Ragtime*, Mr. Weller is here in a deeper, more somber mode, as he chronicles the desperate attempts of a sixteen year-old boy to reconcile his divorced parents. Nobody writes better about disillusionment, about people whose hopes and dreams never quite lived up to reality. In *Moonchildren* and *Loose Ends* Mr. Weller dealt with how the Dream ended up in the sixties and seventies, respecitvely; here, the fuzzy decade of the fifties is explored through the eyes of Martin's parents, ex-thirties radicals who have chosen very different ways to cope with the changed, changing times. Elyse, the mother, is still a bohemian, a rebel without a cause who wants to live for something more than the rent and the price of hamburger, whereas Andrew, the father, has dropped back into the system, and accepted Life As It Is. And Martin is caught between these finally irreconcilable outlooks, unable to bring his parents back together and wondering what path *his* life will take. "Mr. Weller finds in one family's distintegration a paradigm of the postwar collapse of liberal idealism. This is without question Mr. Weller's most intelligent play, always intelligent and at times moving."—N.Y. Times. "Emotionally charged...a touching, lovely work."—N.Y. Post.

(#21294)

SPEED-THE-PLOW
(ADVANCED GROUPS—SERIOUS COMEDY)

By DAVID MAMET
2 men, 1 woman—Two interior. (may be simply suggested).

This is, without a doubt, one of Mamet's best plays (including *American Buffalo* and the stunning, Pulitzer Prize-winning *Glengarry Glen Ross*). Joe Mantegna, Ron Silver and Madonna starred on Broadway in this hilarious and devastating satire of Hollywood, a microcosm of the macrocosm of American culture. Charlie Fox has discovered a terrific vehicle for a certain "hot" male movie star, and has brought it to his "best friend" Bobby Gould, "Head of Production" for a major film company. He coulda taken it across the street but no, he's brought it to Bobby. Both see the script as their ticket to the really big table, where the real power is. The star wants to do it, and all they have to do is "pitch" it to their boss. The screenplay is a mass of typical action-picture cliches, which they have decided to pitch as a "buddy film"—the current "hot commodity." They'll be taking a meeting with the studio boss tomorrow; but tonight, Bobby has bet Charlie $500 that he can seduce Karen, a temp secretary. His ruse: he has given her a novel "by some Eastern sissy writer" which he has been asked to "courtesy-read" before saying thanks-but-no-thanks. Karen reads the novel and comes to Bobby's house that night—to convince him that *this*, and *not* the buddy film, should be the company's next project. Her arguments are convincing—all the more so when she agrees to sleep with Bobby, and experience which is apparently so transmogrifying that, much to Charlie's surprise, the next morning he finds he has to plead with Bobby not to put the buddy film "in turnaround", not to pitch the gloomy "sissy film". "By turns hilarious and chilling...[the] dialogue skyrockets."—N.Y. Times. Mamet's clearest, wittiest play."—N.Y. Daily News. "I laughed and laughed. The play is crammed with wonderful, dazzling, brilliant lines."—N.Y. Post. "There isn't a line that isn't somehow insanely funny or scarily insane."—Newsweek.

(#21281)